The 2018 Los Angeles Chargers Passing Index

Bobby Peters

Copyright © 2019 Robert J Peters

All rights reserved.

ISBN: 9781095082058

DEDICATION

To Michelle and Mason.
To all those who have fostered a love of football in me.

The 2018 Los Angeles Chargers Passing Index

Table of Contents

Introduction 7
Flat Fade 14
2 Man Stick 16
3 Man Stick 18
Dragon 20
Slot Fade 22
Levels 24
Smash 26
Smash – Whip 28
Smash - Return 30
Hitch - Seam 32
Scat 34
Scream (Scat – Seam) 36
Weakside Option Route 38
Deep Hitch – Seam 40
Deep Hitches (comeback from tight split) 42
Dusty 45
Hank Trade 48
Deep Out – Clear Out (2 Man) 50
Deep Out – Clear Out (3 Man) (Train) 52
Backside Spot – Dig 54
Backside Dig – Drag – HB Burst 56
Trips Dig – (high-low #3) 58
"Swirl" Route 60
Post - Wheel 62
Post Wheel – Drive HB Swing Strong 65
Flood (3 man) 67
Flood (4 man & Seattle) 71
H Angle 74
Play Action – Quick Slant 76
Pin/Pull Slants RPO (Pass Thrown) 79
Scissors – Backside Dig 81

Scissors – Corner (Max Protection)	84
Scissors – Corner	87
Slot Scissors	89
Four Verticals	91
Verticals – Drag	93
Verticals - Drive	96
Hank (Full Field)	97
All Curls	99
Drive Variations	102
Shallow Cross	105
Middle Read	108
Y Cross	111
U / X / Z Cross	115
X / Z Cross - Drag	119
Play Action - Dagger	121
Bunch Dagger	124
Bunch Dagger - Whip	125
Bunch Dagger - Drag	126
Post – Comeback Double Move	127
Mesh	128
RB & TE Slow Screens	132
Tunnel Screens	135
Red Zone Play Action Specials	139
Other Misc. Play Calls	142

Introduction

Anthony Lynn and Ken Whisenhunt put together an interesting system for quarterback Philip Rivers in 2018. The system features many concepts that are similar to traditional concepts found everywhere throughout football (think four verticals, dagger, scat, etc.). The Chargers often adjusted one or two routes to give the concept a different look and feel for the quarterback. Often times these adjustments placed additional stress on specific zone defenders, and gave man defenders trouble in getting through extra traffic. The route adjustments also throw off any pattern reading that defenses are accustomed to, based on initial reads and stems. The use of "Post – Wheel Drive HB Swing Strong", "Scream", and "Scissors - Corner" are a few of the many examples of this theme.

The half – field concepts are drawn up individually, with each occasion used labeled in the charts. These concepts were often combined with other half field concepts. The most common variations are listed in each section. For the full – filed concepts, each unique variation was drawn up.

General Notes

- The label "TO" in the charts stands for Turnover.
- The blank down and distance plays are two point conversion attempts.

Top 1st Down Calls

Concept	1st Down Att	1st Down YPP
Hitch - Seam	1	30
Deep Out – Clear Out (2 Man)	3	29.7
"Swirl" Route	4	20.5
Post - Wheel	5	20.4
Play Action - Dagger	2	19.5
Post Wheel – Drive HB Swing Strong	6	16.3
Four Verticals	3	15.3
Verticals – Drag	4	13
Scissors – Corner (Max Protection)	4	12
Shallow Cross	2	12
Mesh	3	11.7
Pin/Pull Slants RPO (Pass Thrown)	5	11.4
U / X / Z Cross	20	11.4
Trips Dig – (high-low #3)	3	11
Smash	5	10.4
Backside Dig – Drag – HB Burst	2	10
Tunnel Screens	4	9.8
Drive Variations	3	9.3
Slot Scissors	5	8.8

Common 1st Down Calls

Concept	1st Down Att	1st Down YPP
U / X / Z Cross	20	11.4
Deep Hitch – Seam	12	3.9
2 Man Stick	9	8.2
Y Cross	7	5.3
Slot Fade	7	4.9
Post Wheel – Drive HB Swing Strong	6	16.3
Flood (3 man)	6	7.7
Scissors – Corner	6	7.3
Weakside Option Route	6	6.5
3 Man Stick	6	6.2
Hank Trade	6	5.5
Dragon	6	4.5

The 2018 Los Angeles Chargers Passing Index

Most Efficient 3rd Down Calls

Concept	3rd Down Att	3rd Down %
Scat	2	100%
Smash – Whip	2	100%
Bunch Dagger - Drag	1	100%
Y Cross	3	67%
Trips Dig – (high-low #3)	3	67%
Middle Read	6	67%
Dusty	6	67%
All Curls	3	67%
Verticals – Drag	8	63%
Mesh	8	63%
Flood (3 man)	5	60%
"Swirl" Route	6	50%
Deep Out – Clear Out (2 Man)	4	50%
Deep Out – Clear Out (3 Man) (Train)	4	50%
Bunch Dagger	2	50%
Bunch Dagger - Whip	4	50%

Most Common 3rd Down Calls

Concept	3rd Down Att	3rd Down %
Drive Variations	9	33%
Verticals – Drag	8	63%
Mesh	8	63%
Backside Spot – Dig	8	38%
Tunnel Screens	7	29%
Four Verticals	7	0%
Middle Read	6	67%
Dusty	6	67%
"Swirl" Route	6	50%
Smash	6	33%
Flood (3 man)	5	60%
Scissors – Backside Dig	5	40%
Shallow Cross	5	40%
Smash - Return	5	40%
Hank (Full Field)	5	20%

Most Efficient 2nd 6- Calls

Concept	2nd 6- Att	2nd 6- YPP
Scissors – Corner	1	31
Scissors – Corner (Max Protection)	2	31
Hitch - Seam	1	28
X / Z Cross - Drag	1	22
Post – Comeback Double Move	1	17
"Swirl" Route	1	16
Trips Dig – (high-low #3)	2	11.5
RB & TE Slow Screens	3	11.3
Deep Out – Clear Out (2 Man)	1	11

Most Common 2nd 6- Calls

Concept	2nd 6- Att	2nd 6- YPP
RB & TE Slow Screens	3	11.3
Deep Hitches (comeback from tight split)	3	3.7
Dragon	3	3
Shallow Cross	3	-2.7
Scissors – Corner (Max Protection)	2	31
Trips Dig – (high-low #3)	2	11.5
H Angle	2	9.5
Deep Hitch – Seam	2	9
Play Action - Dagger	2	8.5
Slot Fade	2	5.5
2 Man Stick	2	5.5
Hank Trade	2	4
Backside Dig – Drag – HB Burst	2	-2.5

The 2018 Los Angeles Chargers Passing Index

Most Efficient 2nd 7+ Calls

Concept	2nd 7+ Att	2nd 7+ YPP
"Swirl" Route	1	30
Scream (Scat – Seam)	4	26.3
Bunch Dagger - Drag	1	23
Deep Hitches (comeback from tight split)	6	22.5
Slot Fade	3	16.7
U / X / Z Cross	4	16.5
H Angle	1	16
Levels	4	14.5
Backside Spot – Dig	1	12
Play Action - Dagger	2	11.5

Most Common 2nd 7+ Calls

Concept	2nd 7+ Att	2nd 7+ YPP
Hank Trade	9	6.7
RB & TE Slow Screens	8	7.6
2 Man Stick	7	6.6
Deep Hitches (comeback from tight split)	6	22.5
Scissors – Corner	5	9.8
Hitch - Seam	5	9.4
Backside Dig – Drag – HB Burst	5	6.8
Scream (Scat – Seam)	4	26.3
U / X / Z Cross	4	16.5
Levels	4	14.5
Post - Wheel	4	9.5
Flat Fade	4	7.5
Weakside Option Route	4	6.5
Shallow Cross	4	6.3
Dragon	4	6
Drive Variations	4	6
Hank (Full Field)	4	5.8
Deep Hitch – Seam	4	4.5
Trips Dig – (high-low #3)	4	4.3

Most Efficient Red Zone 10-0 Calls

Concept	Red Zone 10-0 Att	Red Zone 0-10 %
Hank (Full Field)	1	100%
Trips Dig – (high-low #3)	1	100%
Play Action – Quick Slant	3	67%
Dusty	6	50%
"Swirl" Route	2	50%
Smash – Whip	2	50%
Smash - Return	7	43%
Red Zone Play Action Specials	11	36%
Backside Spot – Dig	3	33%
Scat	4	25%

Most Common Red Zone 10-0 Calls

Concept	Red Zone 10-0 Att	Red Zone 0-10 %
Red Zone Play Action Specials	11	36%
Smash - Return	7	43%
Dusty	6	50%
Smash	5	0%
Scat	4	25%
Play Action – Quick Slant	3	67%
Backside Spot – Dig	3	33%
Verticals - Drive	3	0%

Most Efficient Red Zone 10-20 Calls

Concept	Red Zone 11-20 Att	Red Zone 11-20 %
Scream (Scat – Seam)	1	100%
Dusty	2	50%
Backside Spot – Dig	2	50%
Smash	2	50%
Deep Hitches (comeback from tight split)	2	50%
Post - Wheel	2	50%
RB & TE Slow Screens	5	20%

Most Common Red Zone 10-20 Calls

Concept	Red Zone 11-20 Att	Red Zone 11-20 %
RB & TE Slow Screens	5	20%
Smash - Return	4	0%
Dusty	2	50%
Backside Spot – Dig	2	50%
Smash	2	50%
Deep Hitches (comeback from tight split)	2	50%
Post - Wheel	2	50%
Scat	2	0%
Four Verticals	2	0%
H Angle	2	0%

Flat Fade

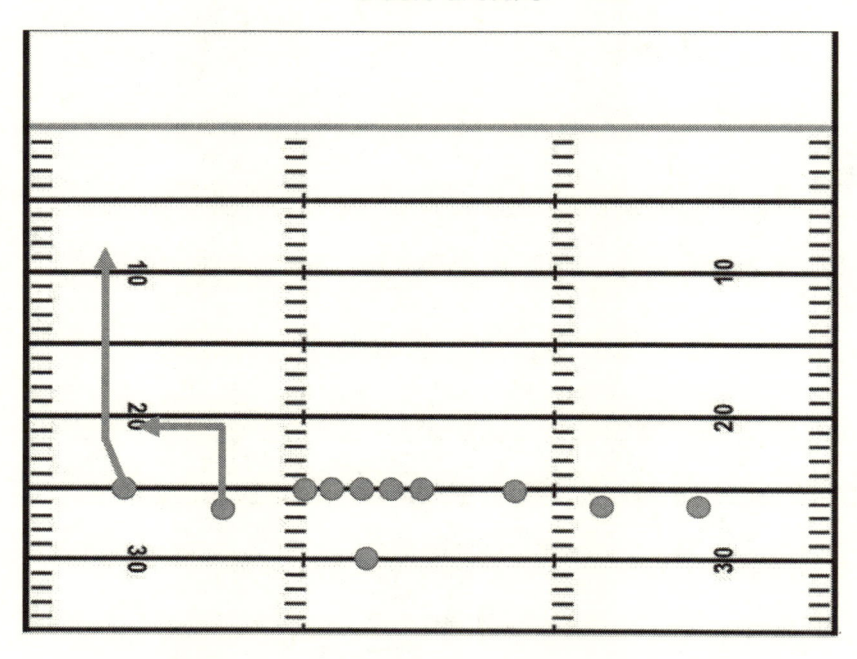

Average Yards per Play	6.5

1st Down	
Called	Average
5	6.6
2nd Down 6-1	
Called	Average
1	0.0
Red Zone 10-0	
Called	Touchdown %
0	0%

Third Down (includes RZ)	
Called	Success Rate
1	0%
2nd Down 7+	
Called	Average
4	7.5
Red Zone 10-20	
Called	Touchdown %
1	0%

The 2018 Los Angeles Chargers Passing Index

Week	Quarter	Time	Down	ToGo	Location	Yards
Week 2 vs BUF	1	15:00	1	10	LAC 25	7
Week 2 vs BUF	2	8:36	2	10	LAC 19	11
Week 2 vs BUF	2	4:15	2	7	BUF 17	14
Week 2 vs BUF	4	9:57	2	7	BUF 47	7
Week 3 vs LAR	2	7:44	1	10	LAC 25	0
Week 5 vs OAK	1	11:52	3	5	RAI 25	-6
Week 11 vs DEN	3	8:38	1	10	LAC 22	7
Week 14 vs CIN	1	13:42	1	10	LAC 48	19
Week 15 vs KC	1	14:14	2	6	LAC 24	TO
Week 15 vs KC	4	5:55	1	10	KAN 23	0
WC vs BAL	2	6:42	2	16	LAC 49	12

Most Often Paired With:

- 3 Man Stick

2 Man Stick

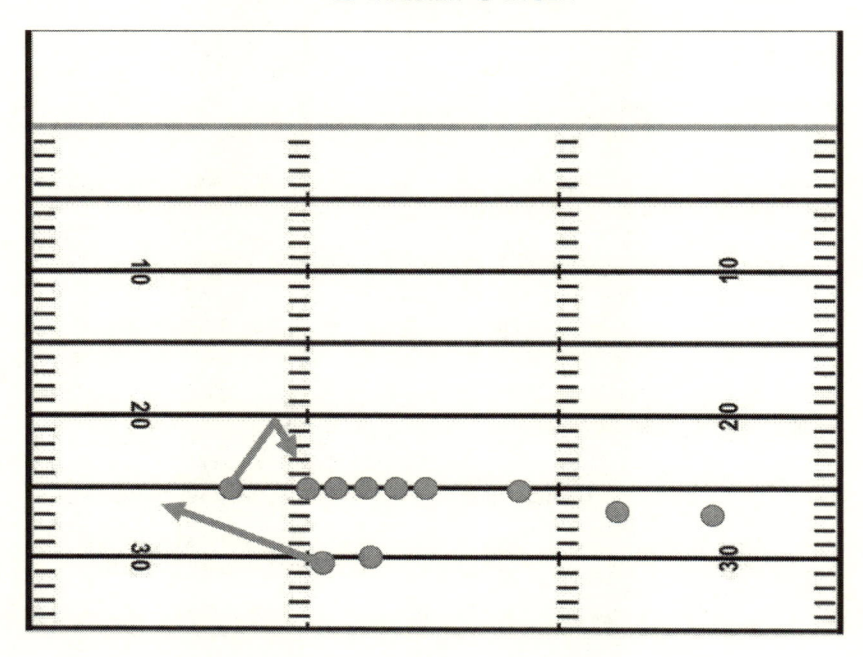

Average Yards per Play	6.1

1st Down	
Called	Average
9	8.2
2nd Down 6-1	
Called	Average
2	5.5
Red Zone 10-0	
Called	Touchdown %
1	0%

Third Down (includes RZ)	
Called	Success Rate
3	33%
2nd Down 7+	
Called	Average
7	6.6
Red Zone 10-20	
Called	Touchdown %
0	0%

The 2018 Los Angeles Chargers Passing Index

Week	Quarter	Time	Down	ToGo	Location	Yards
Week 5 vs OAK	2	4:14	1	10	RAI 44	44
Week 6 vs CLE	2	12:47	1	10	LAC 25	5
Week 7 vs TEN	4	7:36	2	11	LAC 40	0
Week 11 vs DEN	2	0:56	1	10	LAC 9	8
Week 11 vs DEN	3	1:01	3	1	LAC 35	0
Week 12 vs ARI	2	8:58	2	17	LAC 29	18
Week 12 vs ARI	3	2:23	2	9	CRD 23	5
Week 13 vs PIT	2	2:40	1	10	LAC 25	6
Week 13 vs PIT	2	2:10	2	4	LAC 31	8
Week 13 vs PIT	3	9:06	2	5	LAC 17	3
Week 13 vs PIT	4	4:10	1	10	LAC 25	0
Week 17 vs DEN	1	5:06	2	10	LAC 42	2
WC vs BAL	1	11:08	3	2	LAC 31	-1
WC vs BAL	2	1:12	3	1	LAC 35	5
WC vs BAL	3	14:48	1	10	RAV 26	0
DIV vs NE	2	1:36	2	20	LAC 15	10

Most Often Paired With:

- Hank Trade
- Slot Fade

3 Man Stick

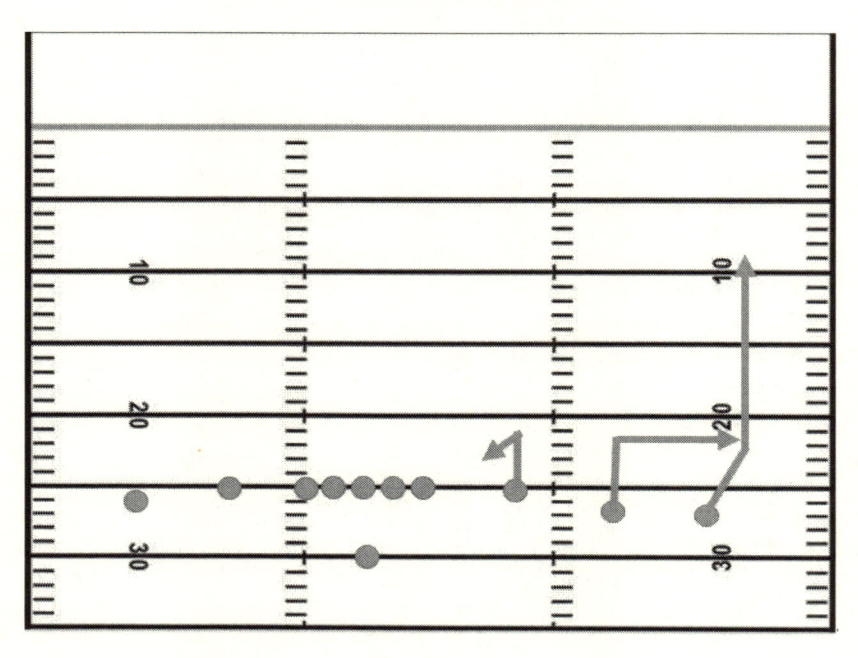

Average Yards per Play	7.7

1st Down		Third Down (includes RZ)	
Called	Average	Called	Success Rate
6	6.2	0	0%
2nd Down 6-1		2nd Down 7+	
Called	Average	Called	Average
0	0.0	2	9.0
Red Zone 10-0		Red Zone 10-20	
Called	Touchdown %	Called	Touchdown %
0	0%	1	0%

The 2018 Los Angeles Chargers Passing Index

Week	Quarter	Time	Down	ToGo	Location	Yards
Week 6 vs CLE	2	12:47	1	10	LAC 25	5
Week 2 vs BUF	1	15:00	1	10	LAC 25	7
Week 2 vs BUF	2	8:36	2	10	LAC 19	11
Week 2 vs BUF	2	4:15	2	7	BUF 17	14
Week 2 vs BUF	4	9:57	2	7	BUF 47	7
Week 5 vs OAK	1	13:06	1	10	RAI 30	0
Week 10 vs OAK	3	14:54	1	10	LAC 23	7
Week 13 vs PIT	3	9:50	1	10	LAC 12	5
Week 17 vs DEN	2	11:34	1	10	LAC 22	13

Most Often Paired With:

- Flat Fade
- Weak Side Option

Dragon

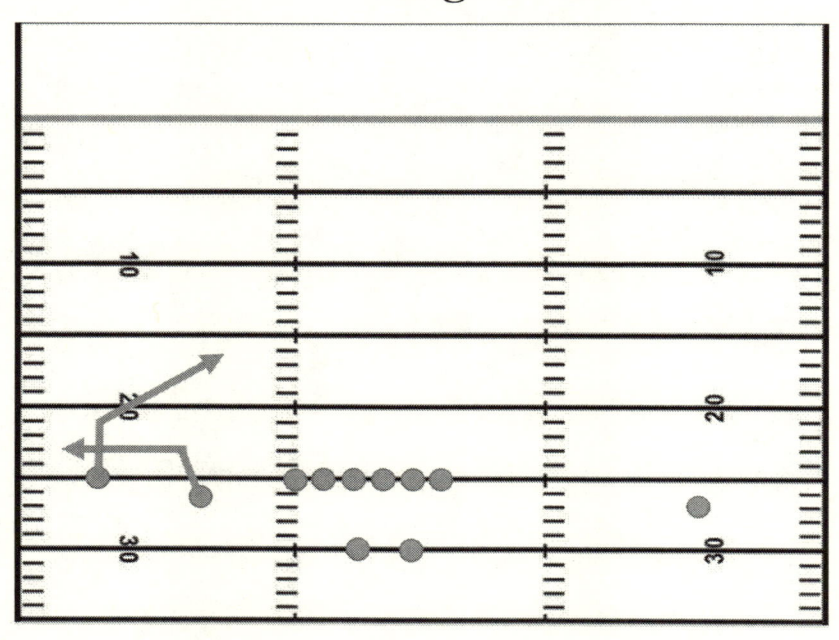

Average Yards per Play   4.2

1st Down		Third Down (includes RZ)	
Called	Average	Called	Success Rate
6	4.5	1	0%
2nd Down 6-1		**2nd Down 7+**	
Called	Average	Called	Average
3	3.0	4	6.0
Red Zone 10-0		**Red Zone 10-20**	
Called	Touchdown %	Called	Touchdown %
0	0%	1	0%

The 2018 Los Angeles Chargers Passing Index

Week	Quarter	Time	Down	ToGo	Location	Yards
Week 1 vs KC	4	7:42	2	1	LAC 48	7
Week 5 vs OAK	2	11:49	3	5	LAC 29	3
Week 6 vs CLE	2	1:53	1	10	CLE 47	14
Week 11 vs DEN	2	6:53	1	10	LAC 16	10
Week 11 vs DEN	2	0:30	2	2	LAC 17	-3
Week 12 vs ARI	2	0:29	1	10	CRD 30	3
Week 15 vs KC	2	13:43	2	7	KAN 22	6
Week 15 vs KC	4	5:55	1	10	KAN 23	0
Week 15 vs KC	4	2:03	1	10	KAN 39	0
Week 16 vs BAL	2	11:31	2	8	LAC 5	9
Week 16 vs BAL	2	1:12	2	10	LAC 39	9
Week 16 vs BAL	2	0:59	1	10	RAV 20	0
Week 17 vs DEN	4	13:19	2	7	LAC 31	0
WC vs BAL	2	1:17	2	6	LAC 30	5
DIV vs NE	3	6:23	1	10	LAC 28	0

Dragon was a mirrored concept for the Chargers in 2018.

Slot Fade

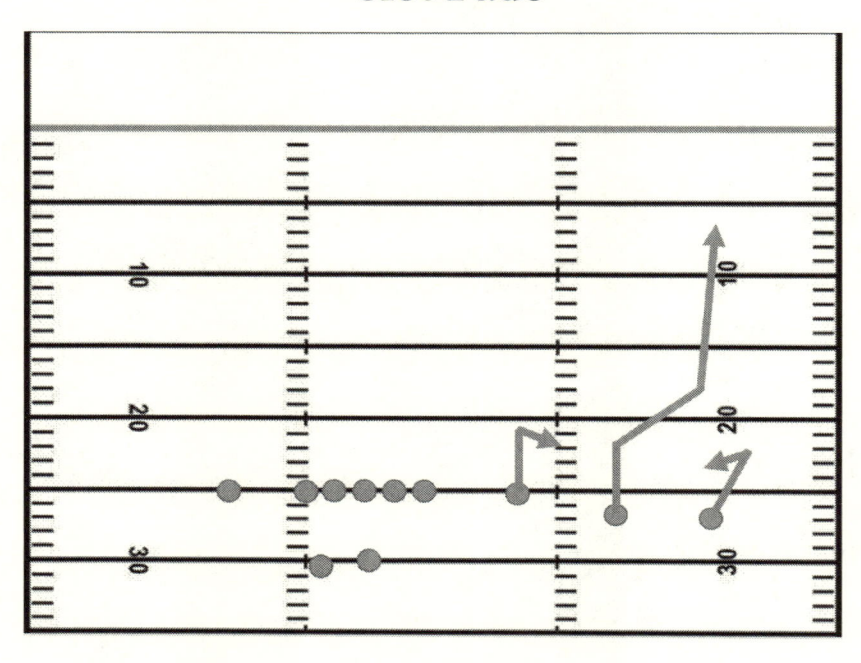

Average Yards per Play	6.7

1st Down	
Called	Average
7	4.9
2nd Down 6-1	
Called	Average
2	5.5
Red Zone 10-0	
Called	Touchdown %
0	0%

Third Down (includes RZ)	
Called	Success Rate
4	25%
2nd Down 7+	
Called	Average
3	16.7
Red Zone 10-20	
Called	Touchdown %
1	0%

The 2018 Los Angeles Chargers Passing Index

Week	Quarter	Time	Down	ToGo	Location	Yards
Week 3 vs LAR	2	15:00	3	6	LAC 29	0
Week 3 vs LAR	3	13:38	1	10	LAC 44	10
Week 4 vs SF	2	0:53	3	3	SFO 22	22
Week 4 vs SF	3	12:38	2	8	SFO 49	24
Week 6 vs CLE	1	0:54	1	10	LAC 4	0
Week 13 vs PIT	2	2:40	1	10	LAC 25	6
Week 6 vs CLE	3	6:23	1	15	LAC 40	0
Week 7 vs TEN	2	12:05	2	8	LAC 20	26
Week 13 vs PIT	2	2:10	2	4	LAC 31	8
Week 11 vs DEN	1	4:00	2	10	LAC 18	0
Week 14 vs CIN	3	3:59	1	10	LAC 4	0
Week 14 vs CIN	2	1:51	3	1	LAC 16	-10
Week 14 vs CIN	**4**	**7:54**	**3**	**3**	**CIN 14**	**0**
Week 16 vs BAL	**1**	**12:06**	**2**	**5**	**LAC 30**	**3**
Week 17 vs DEN	1	9:55	1	10	LAC 31	18
DIV vs NE	3	6:23	1	10	LAC 28	0

Most Often Paired With:

- 2 Man Stick
- Quads variations in bold

Levels

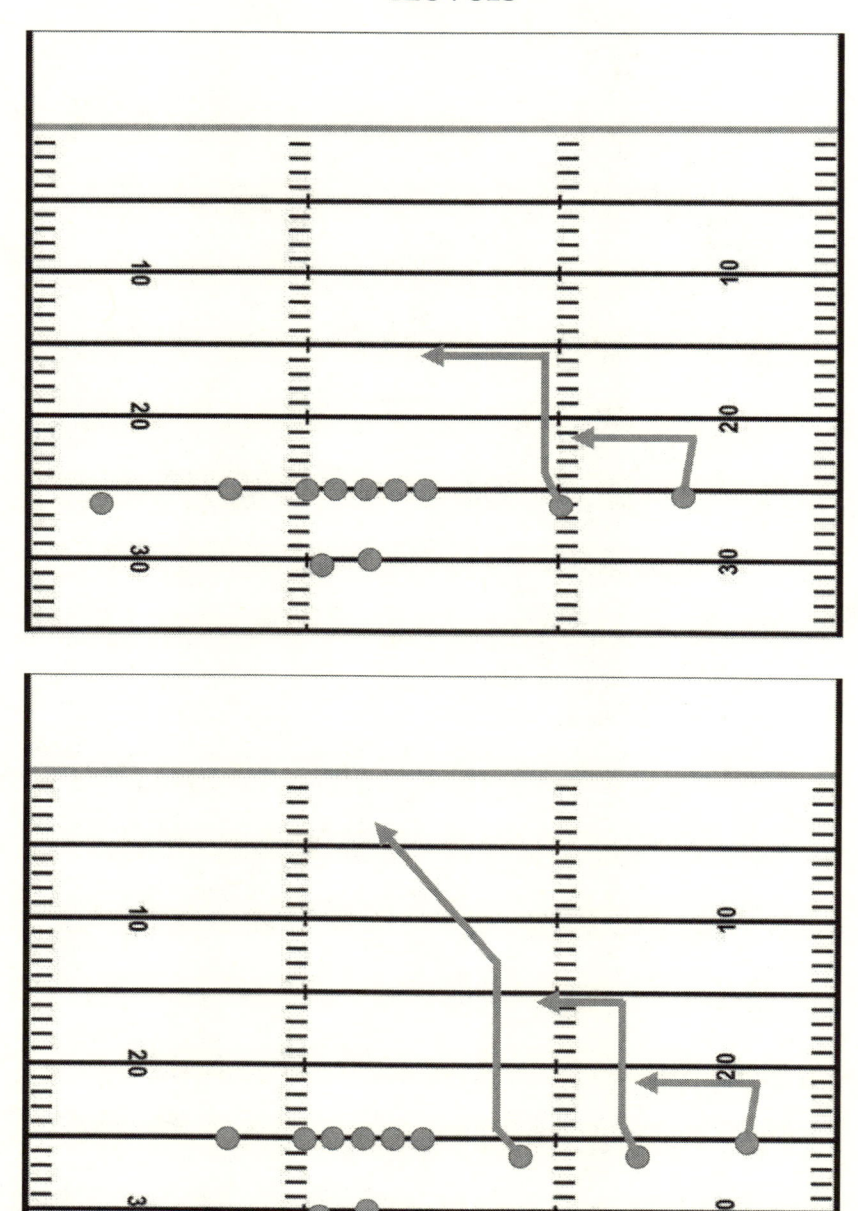

The 2018 Los Angeles Chargers Passing Index

Average Yards per Play	10.7

1st Down		Third Down (includes RZ)	
Called	Average	Called	Success Rate
3	6.0	1	0%
2nd Down 6-1		2nd Down 7+	
Called	Average	Called	Average
1	7.0	4	14.5
Red Zone 10-0		Red Zone 10-20	
Called	Touchdown %	Called	Touchdown %
0	0%	0	0%

Week	Quarter	Time	Down	ToGo	Location	Yards
Week 1 vs KC	3	0:15	1	10	LAC 29	5
Week 1 vs KC	4	13:34	2	4	KAN 35	7
Week 2 vs BUF	**3**	**1:16**	**3**	**17**	**LAC 18**	**13**
Week 4 vs SF	1	11:01	2	8	LAC 39	3
Week 7 vs TEN	3	3:25	1	10	LAC 45	5
Week 9 vs SEA	**2**	**1:55**	**2**	**10**	**LAC 47**	**23**
Week 10 vs OAK	2	0:47	2	12	RAI 25	6
Week 11 vs DEN	3	2:17	1	10	LAC 26	8
Week 15 vs KC	**2**	**5:41**	**2**	**15**	**LAC 30**	**26**

Trips variations in bold

Most Often Paired With

- Verticals with HB Swing to the Vertical side
- Deep Hitch – Seam

Smash

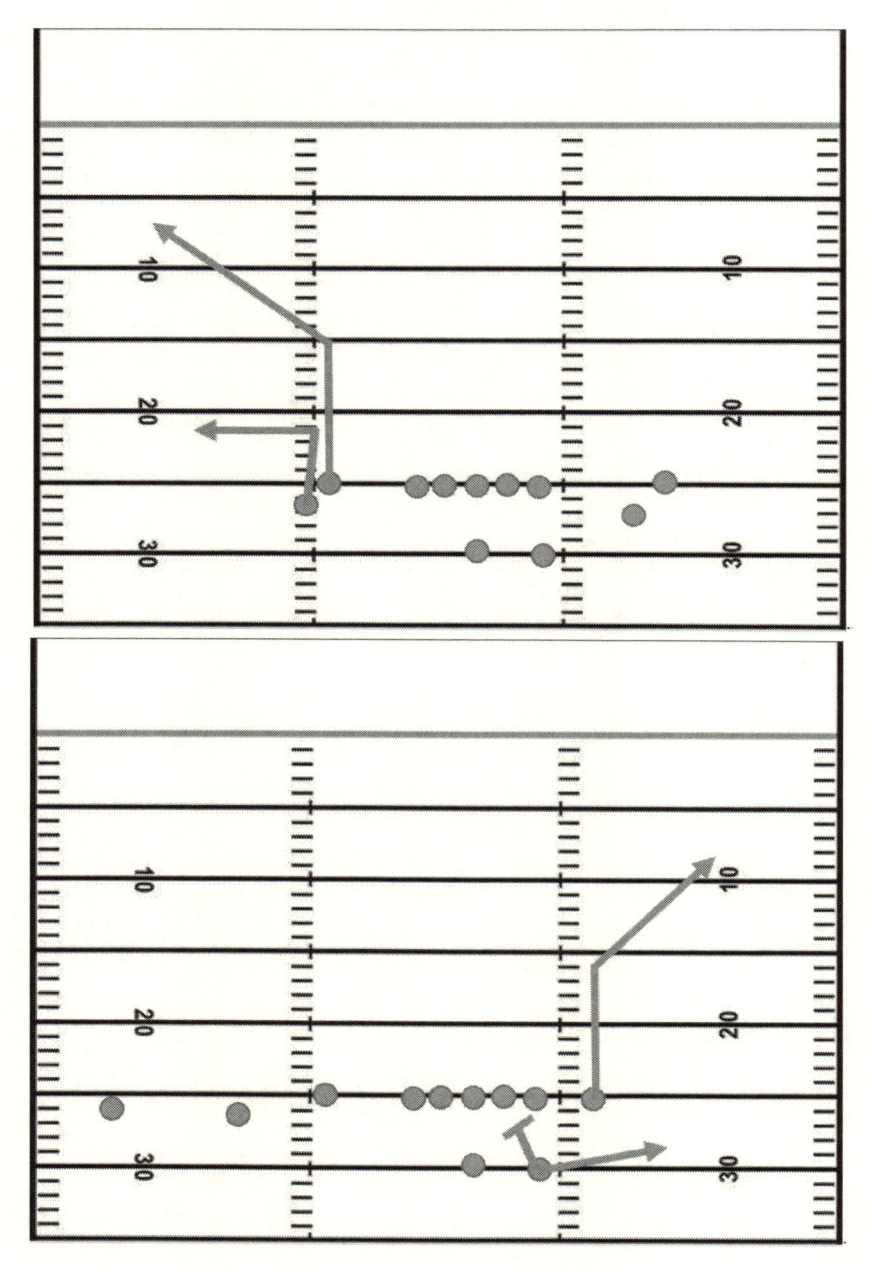

The 2018 Los Angeles Chargers Passing Index

Average Yards per Play	9.2

1st Down	
Called	Average
5	10.4

Third Down (includes RZ)	
Called	Success Rate
6	33%

2nd Down 6-1	
Called	Average
0	0.0

2nd Down 7+	
Called	Average
1	0.0

Red Zone 10-0	
Called	Touchdown %
1	0%

Red Zone 10-20	
Called	Touchdown %
2	50%

Week	Quarter	Time	Down	ToGo	Location	Yards
Week 1 vs KC	2	1:09	3	14	LAC 21	0
Week 1 vs KC	4	5:52	4	2	KAN 27	23
Week 2 vs BUF	1	13:32	3	3	LAC 32	2
Week 2 vs BUF	2	6:38	1	10	LAC 41	22
Week 6 vs CLE	1	10:50	1	10	CLE 21	17
Week 11 vs DEN	2	9:17	2	20	LAC 32	TO
Week 12 vs ARI	2	0:19	3	2	CRD 22	20
Week 13 vs PIT	3	8:18	3	2	LAC 20	21
Week 14 vs CIN	1	11:46	1	10	CIN 14	14
Week 15 vs KC	4	0:39	1	10	KAN 10	0
Week 16 vs BAL	2	2:00	1	10	LAC 39	5
Week 16 vs BAL	2	1:04	1	10	RAV 37	2
Week 16 vs BAL	4	6:51	1	10	RAV 34	6
Week 16 vs BAL	4	5:29	3	5	RAV 29	-11
WC vs BAL	3	7:11	3	6	LAC 29	0
DIV vs NE	3	2:40	2	13	NWE 18	17

Most Often Paired With:

- Verticals

Smash – Whip

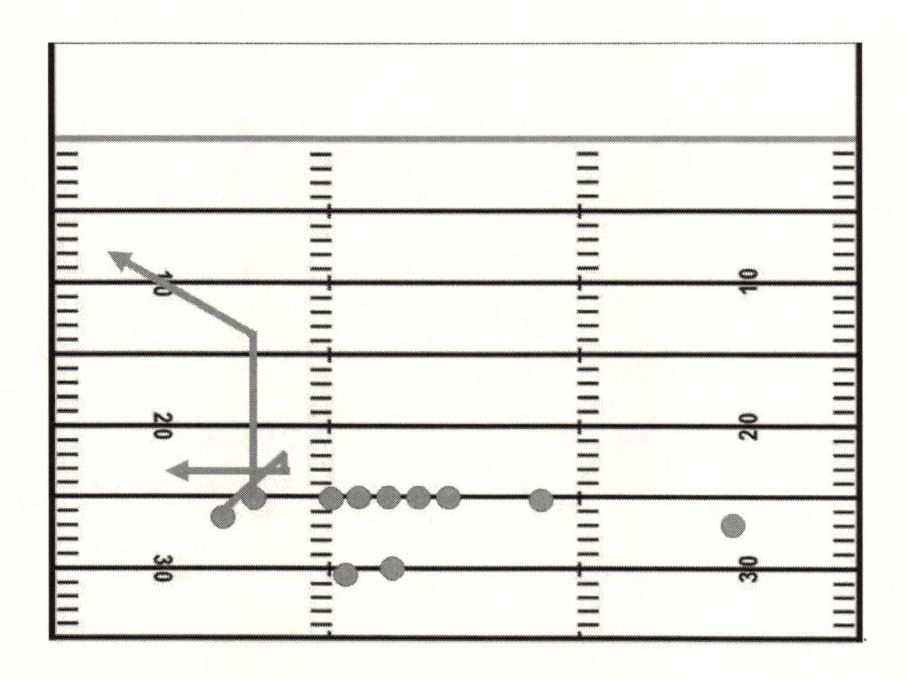

Average Yards per Play	8.8

1st Down		Third Down (includes RZ)	
Called	Average	Called	Success Rate
0	0.0	2	100%
2nd Down 6-1		2nd Down 7+	
Called	Average	Called	Average
0	0.0	0	0.0
Red Zone 10-0		Red Zone 10-20	
Called	Touchdown %	Called	Touchdown %
2	50%	0	0%

The 2018 Los Angeles Chargers Passing Index

Week	Quarter	Time	Down	ToGo	Location	Yards
Week 3 vs LAR	2	6:54	3	4	LAC 31	27
Week 4 vs SF	2	2:03	3	2	SFO 31	2
Week 11 vs DEN	3	11:02	1	8	DEN 8	0
Week 11 vs DEN	3	10:02	1	6	DEN 6	6

Most Often Paired With:

- Scat
- Backside Dig Combos

Smash - Return

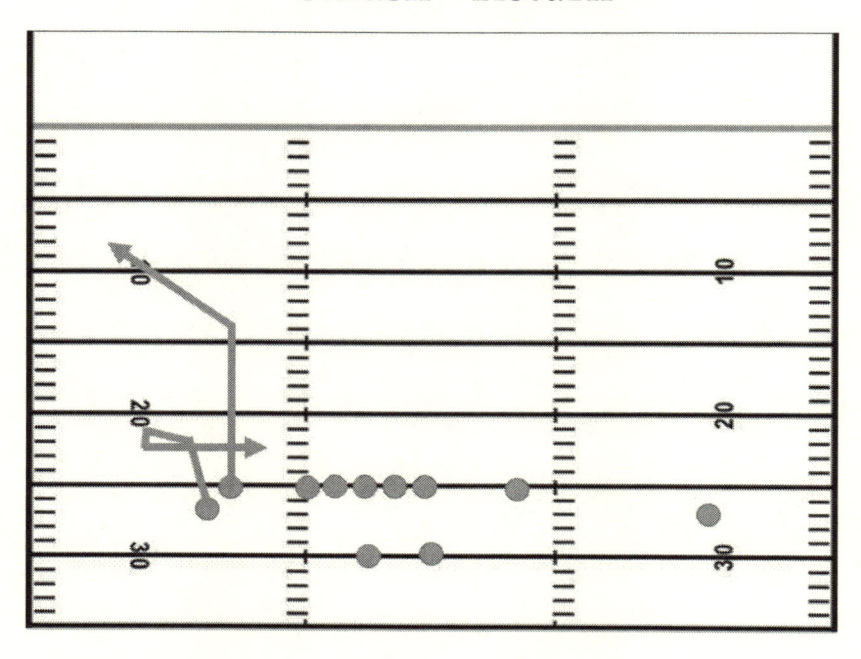

Average Yards per Play	2.4

1st Down	
Called	Average
0	0.0

Third Down (includes RZ)	
Called	Success Rate
5	40%

2nd Down 6-1	
Called	Average
0	0.0

2nd Down 7+	
Called	Average
0	0.0

Red Zone 10-0	
Called	Touchdown %
7	43%

Red Zone 10-20	
Called	Touchdown %
4	0%

The 2018 Los Angeles Chargers Passing Index

Week	Quarter	Time	Down	ToGo	Location	Yards
Week 3 vs LAR	4	11:59	3	8	RAM 8	0
Week 4 vs SF	3	10:40	3	4	SFO 6	6
Week 4 vs SF	3	8:00	2	8	SFO 10	3
Week 4 vs SF	3	7:52	3	5	SFO 7	0
Week 7 vs TEN	1	1:54	3	7	OTI 11	0
Week 11 vs DEN	2	2:45	2	4	DEN 4	4
Week 12 vs ARI	1	0:25	1	13	CRD 13	-1
Week 12 vs ARI	2	14:18	3	9	CRD 9	9
Week 15 vs KC	2	0:57	1	10	KAN 11	0
Week 15 vs KC	2	0:54	2	10	KAN 11	TO
Week 15 vs KC	4	4:38	2	6	KAN 9	3

Most Often Paired With:

- Mirrored
- Scream

Hitch - Seam

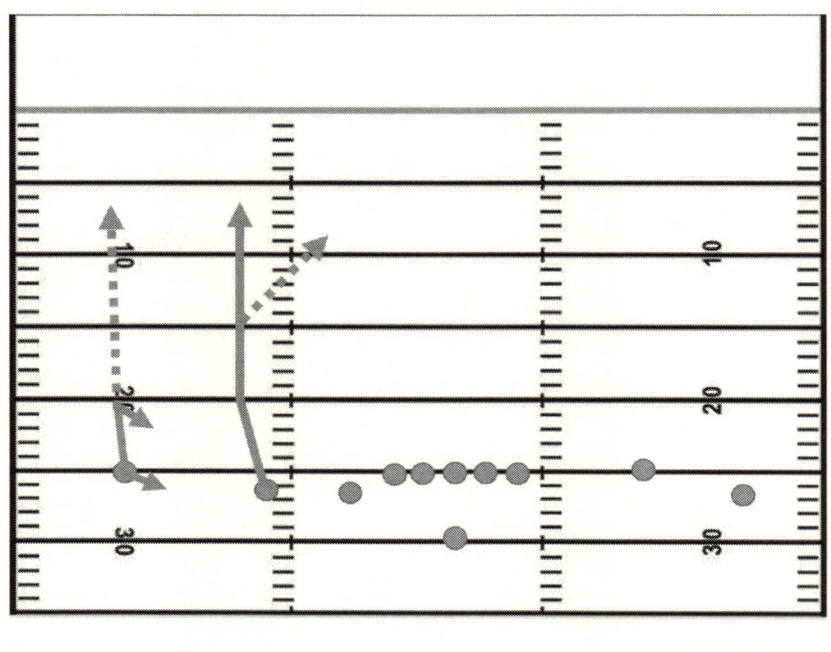

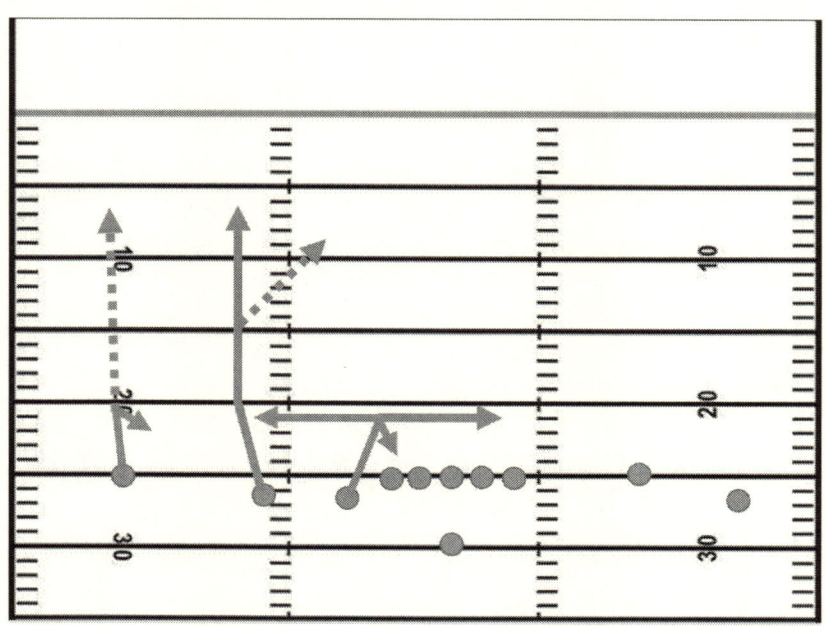

The 2018 Los Angeles Chargers Passing Index

Average Yards per Play	12.1

1st Down		Third Down (includes RZ)	
Called	Average	Called	Success Rate
1	30.0	0	0%
2nd Down 6-1		2nd Down 7+	
Called	Average	Called	Average
1	28.0	5	9.4
Red Zone 10-0		Red Zone 10-20	
Called	Touchdown %	Called	Touchdown %
0	0%	1	0%

Week	Quarter	Time	Down	ToGo	Location	Yards
Week 1 vs KC	1	6:39	1	10	LAC 25	30
Week 3 vs LAR	2	4:35	2	10	RAM 24	9
Week 13 vs PIT	1	13:41	2	10	LAC 39	18
Week 13 vs PIT	3	5:41	2	14	LAC 49	20
Week 15 vs KC	2	12:19	1	10	KAN 13	-8
Week 16 vs BAL	4	14:56	2	10	LAC 23	0
WC vs BAL	3	2:16	2	6	RAV 43	28
DIV vs NE	2	4:40	2	10	LAC 47	0

Primarily Mirrored

Scat

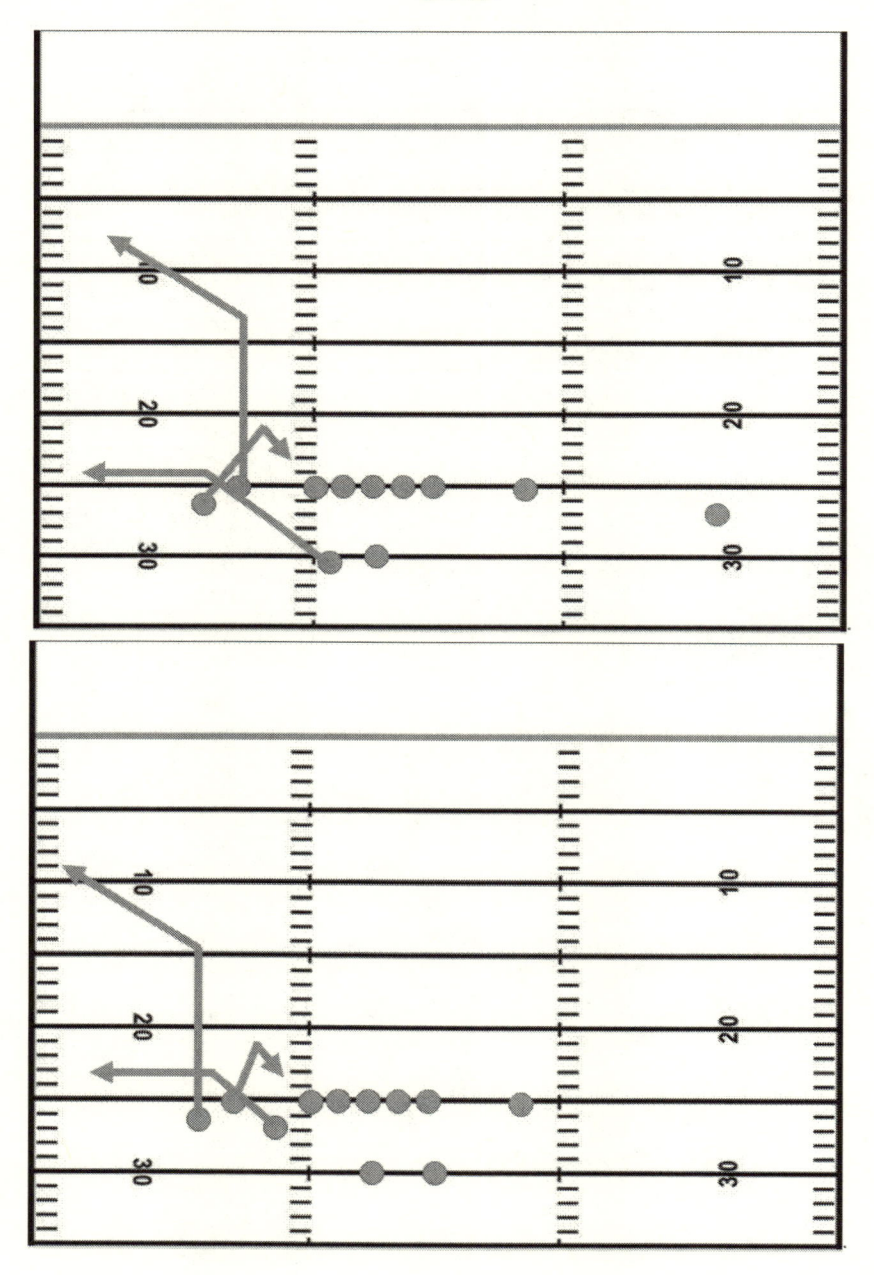

The 2018 Los Angeles Chargers Passing Index

Average Yards per Play	3.3

1st Down		Third Down (includes RZ)	
Called	Average	Called	Success Rate
1	0.0	2	100%

2nd Down 6-1		2nd Down 7+	
Called	Average	Called	Average
0	0.0	0	0.0

Red Zone 10-0		Red Zone 10-20	
Called	Touchdown %	Called	Touchdown %
4	25%	2	0%

Week	Quarter	Time	Down	ToGo	Location	Yards
Week 10 vs OAK	2	0:33	3	1	RAI 14	3
Week 11 vs DEN	3	11:02	1	8	DEN 8	0
Week 11 vs DEN	3	10:02	1	6	DEN 6	6
Week 12 vs ARI	3	8:52	2	5	CRD 9	5
WC vs BAL	3	14:48	1	10	RAV 26	0
Week 15 vs KC	2	0:54	2	10	KAN 11	TO
Week 17 vs DEN	3	4:34	3	3	DEN 9	6

Most Often Paired With
- Smash – Whip
- Smash – Return
- Spot - Dig

Scream (Scat – Seam)

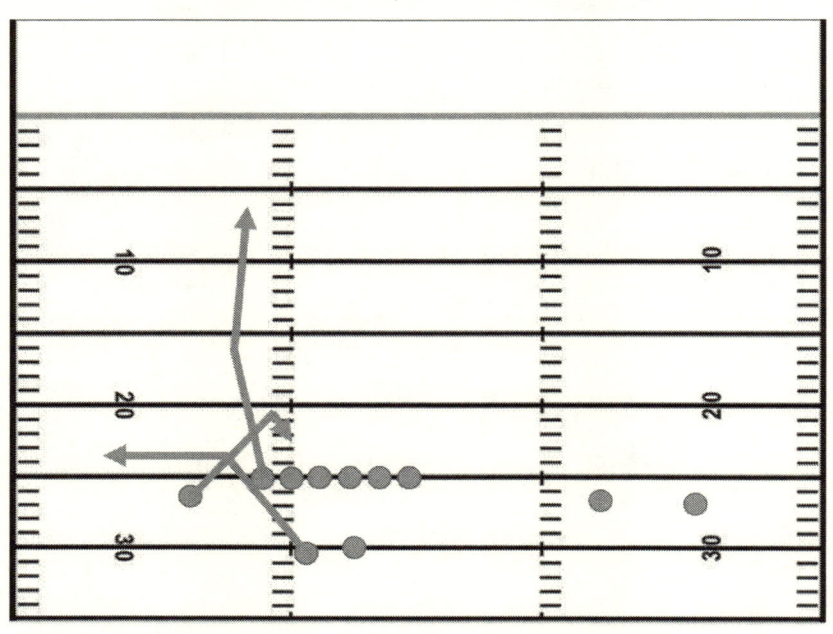

Average Yards per Play	17.0

1st Down		Third Down (includes RZ)	
Called	Average	Called	Success Rate
0	0.0	1	0%
2nd Down 6-1		2nd Down 7+	
Called	Average	Called	Average
0	0.0	4	26.3
Red Zone 10-0		Red Zone 10-20	
Called	Touchdown %	Called	Touchdown %
2	0%	1	100%

The 2018 Los Angeles Chargers Passing Index

Week	Quarter	Time	Down	ToGo	Location	Yards
Week 4 vs SF	3	8:00	2	8	SFO 10	3
Week 4 vs SF	3	7:52	3	5	SFO 7	0
Week 10 vs OAK	2	0:28	1	10	RAI 11	11
Week 10 vs OAK	3	12:43	2	10	LAC 34	66
Week 10 vs OAK	3	5:05	2	9	LAC 12	23
Week 14 vs CIN	3	3:54	2	10	LAC 4	9
Week 15 vs KC	3	1:28	2	10	LAC 34	7

Most Often Paired With:

- Deep Hitches (comeback from tight split)
- Smash - Return

Weakside Option Route

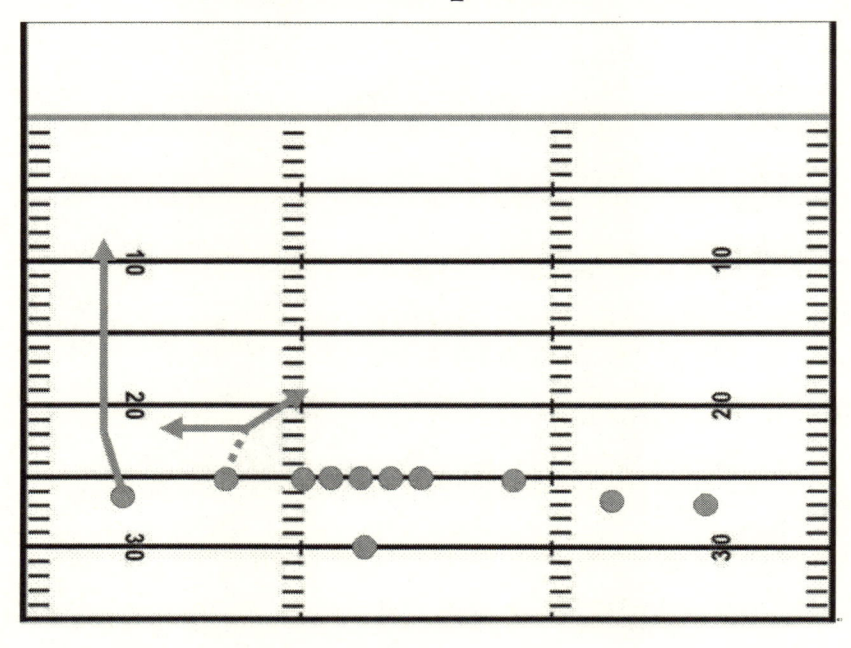

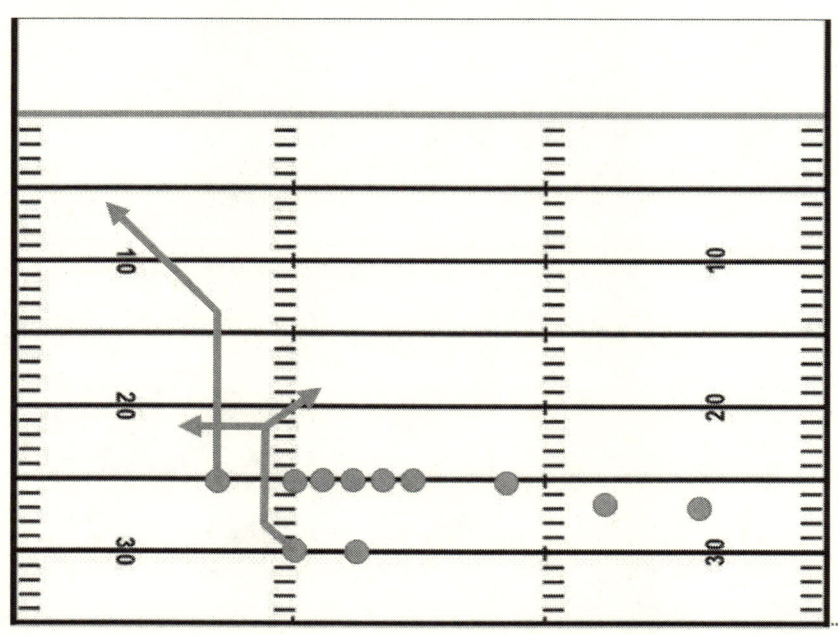

The 2018 Los Angeles Chargers Passing Index

Average Yards per Play	5.6

1st Down	
Called	Average
6	6.5

Third Down (includes RZ)	
Called	Success Rate
2	0%

2nd Down 6-1	
Called	Average
1	7.0

2nd Down 7+	
Called	Average
4	6.5

Red Zone 10-0	
Called	Touchdown %
0	0%

Red Zone 10-20	
Called	Touchdown %
1	0%

Week	Quarter	Time	Down	ToGo	Location	Yards
Week 3 vs LAR	2	4:35	2	10	RAM 24	9
Week 6 vs CLE	1	0:06	3	5	LAC 9	0
Week 7 vs TEN	1	3:24	2	8	OTI 31	17
Week 9 vs SEA	1	1:10	2	8	SEA 13	6
Week 10 vs OAK	3	3:05	3	2	LAC 43	0
Week 11 vs DEN	1	4:00	2	10	LAC 18	0
Week 5 vs OAK	1	13:06	1	10	RAI 30	0
Week 16 vs BAL	2	2:14	2	2	LAC 32	7
Week 17 vs DEN	1	5:57	1	10	LAC 28	14
Week 10 vs OAK	3	14:54	1	10	LAC 23	7
Week 17 vs DEN	3	8:18	1	10	LAC 35	0
Week 13 vs PIT	3	9:50	1	10	LAC 12	5
DIV vs NE	1	0:47	2	9	LAC 26	0
Week 17 vs DEN	2	11:34	1	10	LAC 22	13

Most Often Paired With:

- Trips Dig (high-low #3)
- 3 Man Stick

Deep Hitch – Seam

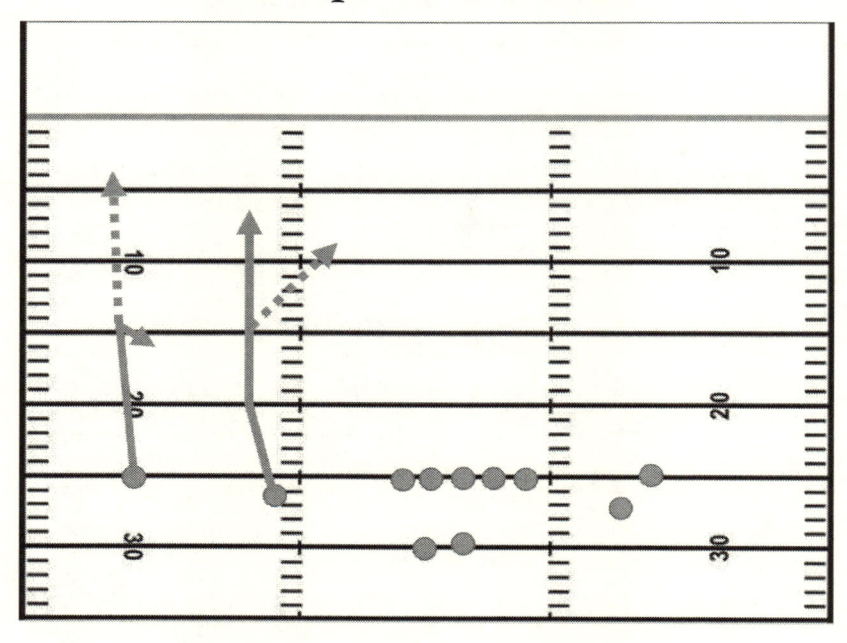

Average Yards per Play	4.9

1st Down		Third Down (includes RZ)	
Called	Average	Called	Success Rate
12	3.9	3	33%
2nd Down 6-1		2nd Down 7+	
Called	Average	Called	Average
2	9.0	4	4.5
Red Zone 10-0		Red Zone 10-20	
Called	Touchdown %	Called	Touchdown %
0	0%	0	0%

The 2018 Los Angeles Chargers Passing Index

Week	Quarter	Time	Down	ToGo	Location	Yards
Week 3 vs LAR	4	5:35	2	10	RAM 22	0
Week 5 vs OAK	2	3:24	1	17	LAC 45	11
Week 5 vs OAK	4	5:10	1	10	RAI 48	3
Week 6 vs CLE	3	9:39	2	3	LAC 26	9
Week 7 vs TEN	3	3:25	1	10	LAC 45	5
Week 10 vs OAK	1	2:00	3	9	LAC 26	0
Week 10 vs OAK	2	0:47	2	12	RAI 25	6
Week 13 vs PIT	4	4:10	1	10	LAC 25	0
Week 11 vs DEN	3	12:15	1	10	DEN 28	15
Week 11 vs DEN	3	8:38	1	10	LAC 22	7
Week 11 vs DEN	3	2:17	1	10	LAC 26	8
Week 12 vs ARI	1	3:18	2	6	CRD 27	9
Week 13 vs PIT	2	2:00	1	10	LAC 39	0
Week 13 vs PIT	3	5:41	2	14	LAC 49	20
Week 13 vs PIT	4	1:12	3	4	PIT 34	12
Week 16 vs BAL	3	10:34	2	19	LAC 28	-8
Week 16 vs BAL	4	2:40	1	10	LAC 25	8
Week 16 vs BAL	4	1:41	1	10	RAV 43	0
Week 17 vs DEN	1	5:08	1	10	LAC 42	0
DIV vs NE	2	1:43	1	10	LAC 25	-10
DIV vs NE	2	1:06	3	10	LAC 25	0
DIV vs NE	3	4:40	2	5	NWE 32	15
DIV vs NE	4	8:32	2	6	NWE 35	2

Most Often Paired With:

- 2 Man Levels
- Backside Dig Combos
- Play Action - Mirrored

Deep Hitches (comeback from tight split)

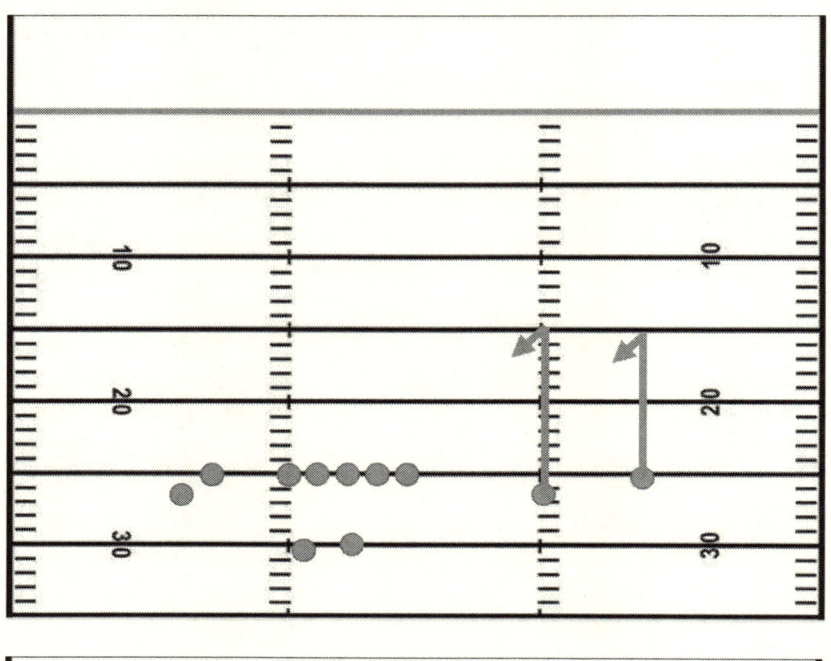

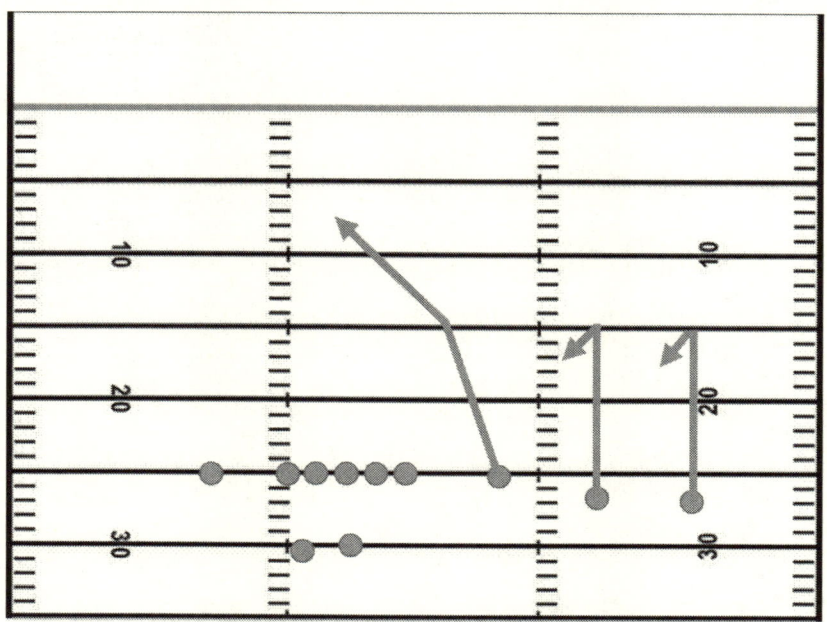

The 2018 Los Angeles Chargers Passing Index

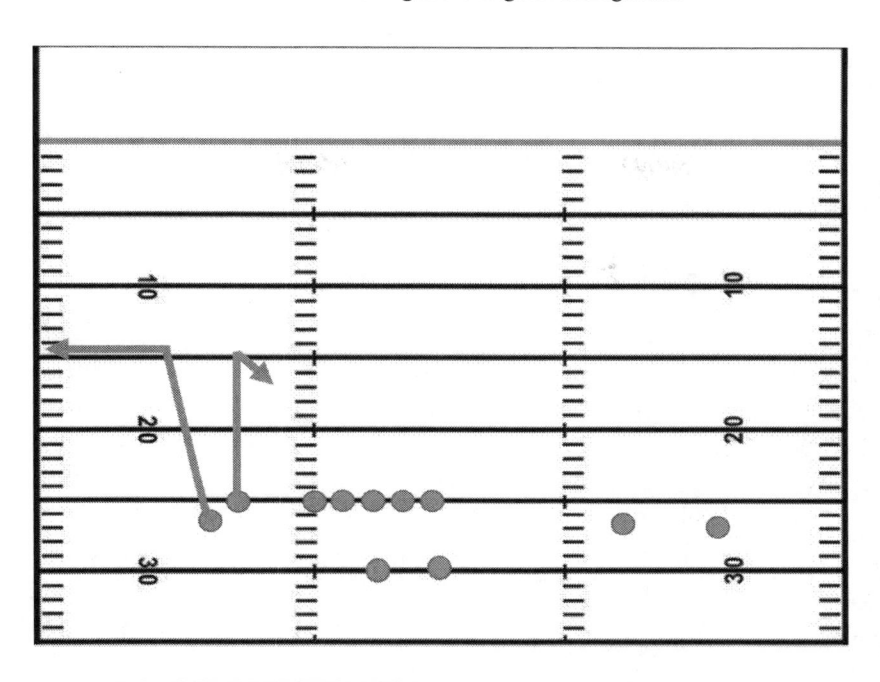

Average Yards per Play	9.9

1st Down		Third Down (includes RZ)	
Called	Average	Called	Success Rate
4	4.3	4	0%
2nd Down 6-1		2nd Down 7+	
Called	Average	Called	Average
3	3.7	6	22.5
Red Zone 10-0		Red Zone 10-20	
Called	Touchdown %	Called	Touchdown %
0	0%	2	50%

Week	Quarter	Time	Down	ToGo	Location	Yards
Week 1 vs KC	4	14:18	1	10	KAN 41	6
Week 2 vs BUF	3	5:33	1	10	LAC 12	0
Week 4 vs SF	3	4:37	2	5	LAC 45	-8
Week 5 vs OAK	4	5:10	1	10	RAI 48	3
Week 7 vs TEN	3	6:45	3	12	LAC 35	11
Week 9 vs SEA	2	9:20	2	10	LAC 24	0
Week 9 vs SEA	2	1:17	2	10	SEA 30	30
Week 9 vs SEA	3	7:24	3	4	SEA 24	0
Week 9 vs SEA	4	1:38	3	7	50	-10
Week 10 vs OAK	2	0:28	1	10	RAI 11	11
Week 10 vs OAK	3	12:43	2	10	LAC 34	66
Week 10 vs OAK	3	5:05	2	9	LAC 12	23
Week 12 vs ARI	2	1:06	1	10	LAC 37	8
Week 12 vs ARI	3	1:41	3	4	CRD 18	3
Week 14 vs CIN	3	3:54	2	10	LAC 4	9
Week 15 vs KC	3	1:28	2	10	LAC 34	7
Week 12 vs ARI	2	1:26	2	2	LAC 28	9
Week 12 vs ARI	2	0:34	2	6	CRD 40	10

Most Often Paired With:

- Scream
- H Angle
- Backside Dig Combos

The 2018 Los Angeles Chargers Passing Index

Dusty

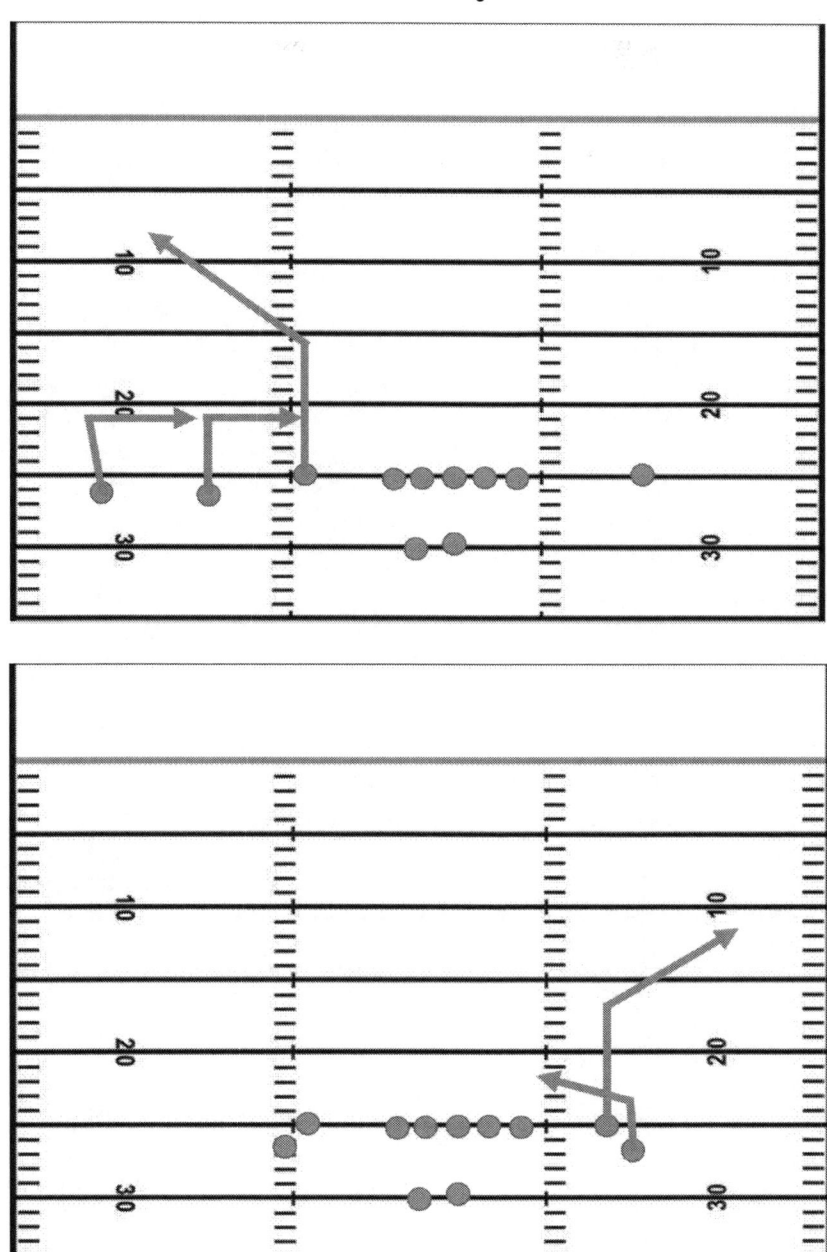

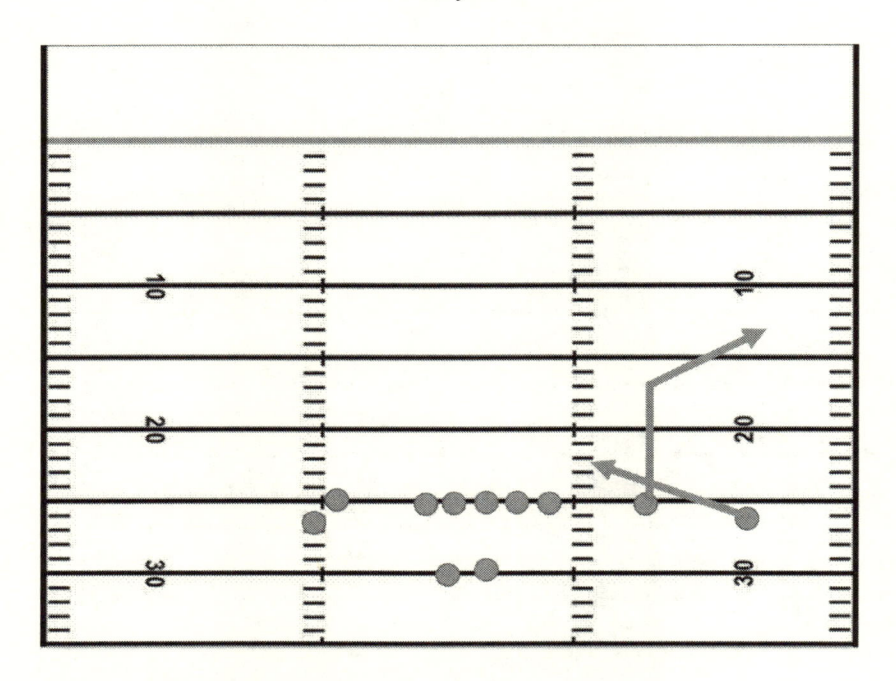

Average Yards per Play	2.6

1st Down		Third Down (includes RZ)	
Called	Average	Called	Success Rate
3	0.0	6	67%
2nd Down 6-1		2nd Down 7+	
Called	Average	Called	Average
0	0.0	2	1.5
Red Zone 10-0		Red Zone 10-20	
Called	Touchdown %	Called	Touchdown %
6	50%	2	50%

The 2018 Los Angeles Chargers Passing Index

Week	Quarter	Time	Down	ToGo	Location	Yards
Week 1 vs KC	2	7:54	2	10	KAN 13	13
Week 3 vs LAR	2	4:41	1	10	RAM 24	0
Week 3 vs LAR	4	12:03	2	8	RAM 8	0
Week 4 vs SF	1	0:48	3	5	SFO 5	5
Week 5 vs OAK	4	4:19	3	6	RAI 44	10
Week 6 vs CLE	4	7:30	3	9	CLE 9	TO
Week 10 vs OAK	1	2:51	1	10	LAC 25	0
Week 11 vs DEN	2	2:50	1	4	DEN 4	0
Week 12 vs ARI	3	11:03	3	6	CRD 41	8
Week 13 vs PIT	2	1:56	2	10	LAC 39	0
Week 13 vs PIT	3	7:41	1	10	LAC 41	0
Week 15 vs KC	2	9:50	2	3	KAN 3	3
Week 15 vs KC	4	1:59	2	10	KAN 39	3
Week 15 vs KC	4	0:04			KAN 2	2
Week 16 vs BAL	2	0:50	3	10	RAV 20	0
DIV vs NE	2	9:25	3	10	LAC 49	0
DIV vs NE	3	3:34	2	13	NWE 20	0
DIV vs NE	4	9:11	1	10	LAC 49	0

Most Often Paired With

- Backside Dig Combos

Hank Trade

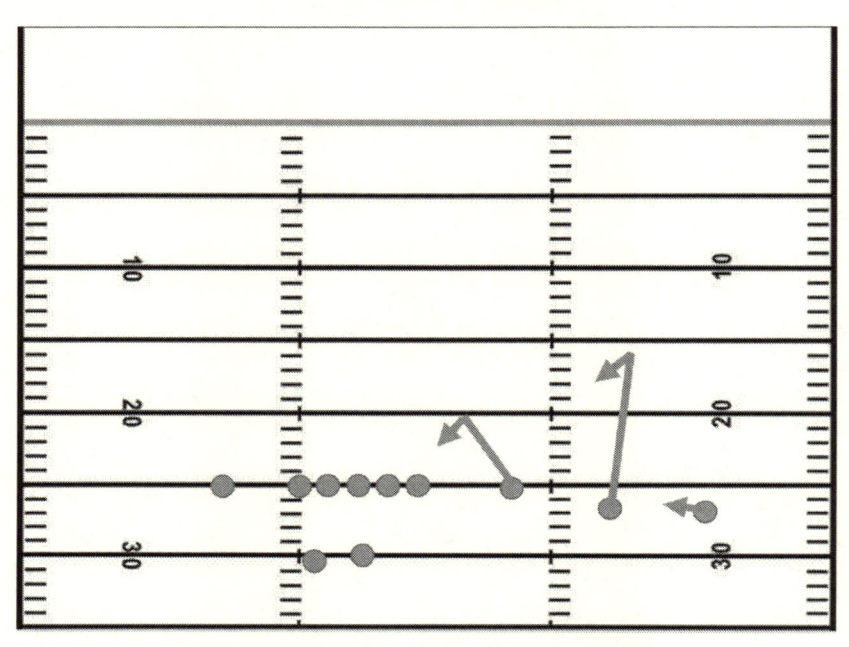

Average Yards per Play	5.9

1st Down		Third Down (includes RZ)	
Called	Average	Called	Success Rate
6	5.5	0	0%
2nd Down 6-1		**2nd Down 7+**	
Called	Average	Called	Average
2	4.0	9	6.7
Red Zone 10-0		**Red Zone 10-20**	
Called	Touchdown %	Called	Touchdown %
0	0%	0	0%

The 2018 Los Angeles Chargers Passing Index

Week	Quarter	Time	Down	ToGo	Location	Yards
Week 6 vs CLE	2	12:47	1	10	LAC 25	5
Week 11 vs DEN	2	0:56	1	10	LAC 9	8
Week 3 vs LAR	4	5:35	2	10	RAM 22	0
Week 4 vs SF	2	1:58	1	10	SFO 29	3
Week 4 vs SF	2	0:08	2	8	SFO 30	0
Week 12 vs ARI	2	8:58	2	17	LAC 29	18
Week 12 vs ARI	3	2:23	2	9	CRD 23	5
Week 13 vs PIT	3	9:06	2	5	LAC 17	3
Week 13 vs PIT	4	1:17	2	7	PIT 37	3
Week 14 vs CIN	2	2:01	1	10	LAC 7	9
Week 12 vs ARI	2	1:45	1	10	LAC 20	8
Week 15 vs KC	4	7:42	2	10	LAC 39	8
Week 17 vs DEN	1	5:06	2	10	LAC 42	2
DIV vs NE	2	1:36	2	20	LAC 15	10
Week 13 vs PIT	4	8:55	2	5	PIT 23	5
Week 14 vs CIN	2	4:55	1	10	LAC 17	0
Week 17 vs DEN	4	7:11	2	19	DEN 36	14

Most often paired with
- Stick
- Mirrored (empty)

Deep Out – Clear Out (2 Man)

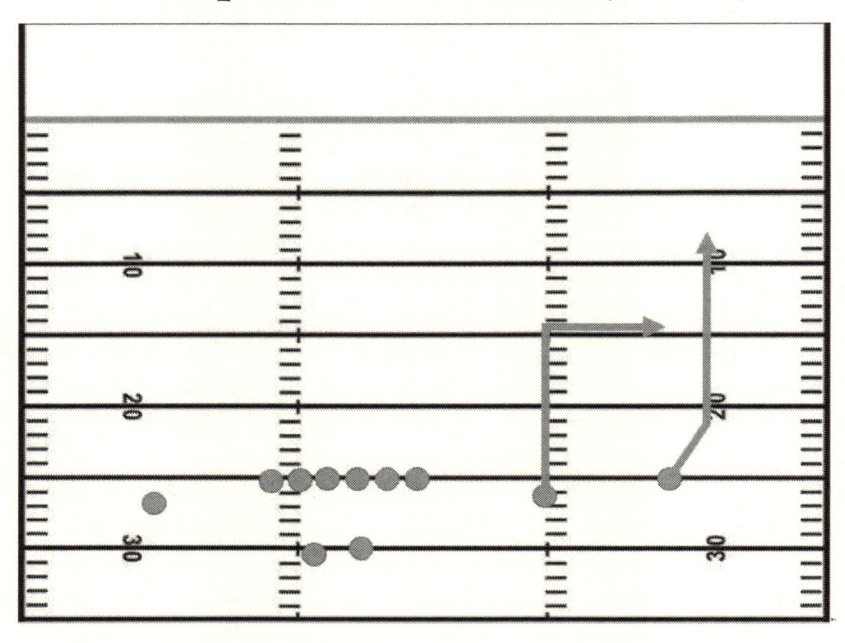

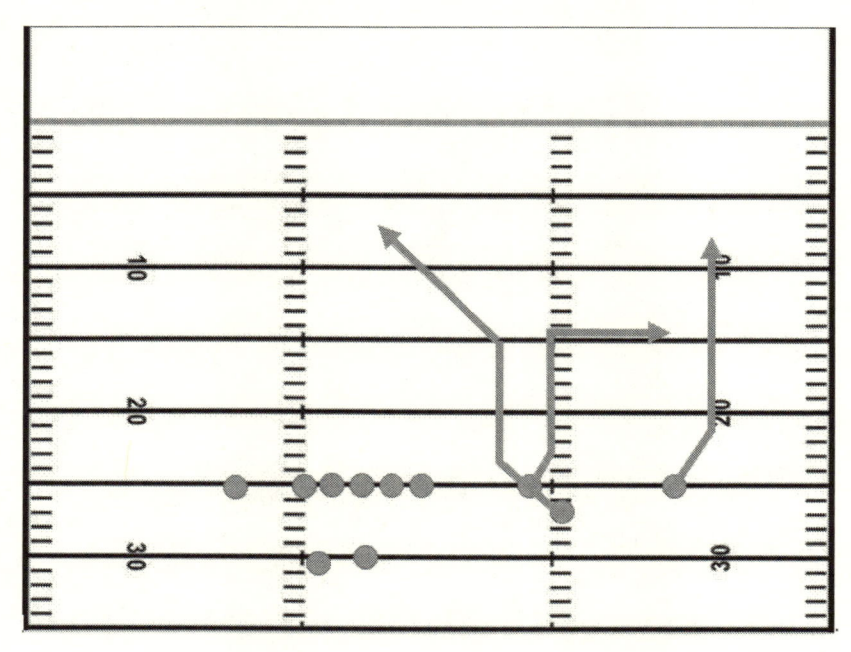

The 2018 Los Angeles Chargers Passing Index

Average Yards per Play	13.4

1st Down		Third Down (includes RZ)	
Called	Average	Called	Success Rate
3	29.7	4	50%

2nd Down 6-1		2nd Down 7+	
Called	Average	Called	Average
1	11.0	2	8.0

Red Zone 10-0		Red Zone 10-20	
Called	Touchdown %	Called	Touchdown %
0	0%	0	0%

Week	Quarter	Time	Down	ToGo	Location	Yards
Week 3 vs LAR	3	11:51	3	8	LAC 27	13
Week 4 vs SF	4	12:04	2	2	LAC 33	11
Week 6 vs CLE	2	1:47	1	10	CLE 33	0
Week 7 vs TEN	1	9:44	1	10	LAC 25	75
Week 9 vs SEA	2	9:20	2	10	LAC 24	0
Week 13 vs PIT	1	15:00	1	10	LAC 25	14
Week 1 vs KC	4	2:56	2	10	LAC 14	16
Week 14 vs CIN	2	4:09	3	10	LAC 17	0
Week 16 vs BAL	3	0:22	3	4	LAC 18	5
Week 16 vs BAL	4	14:52	3	10	LAC 23	0

Most Often Paired With

- Drive Combos and Drag Routes
- Whip (trips version in week 3)

Deep Out – Clear Out (3 Man) (Train)

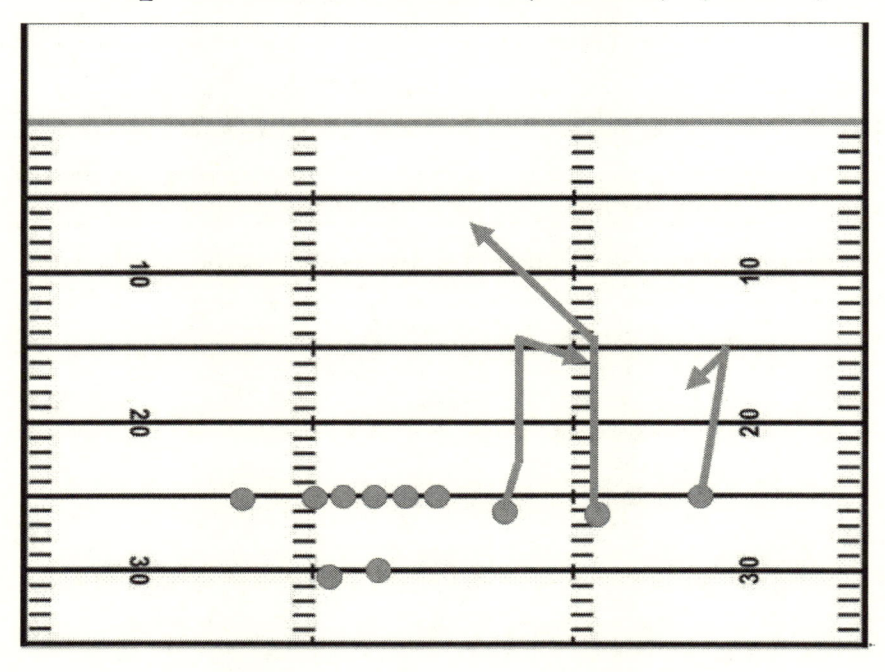

Average Yards per Play	8.5

1st Down		Third Down (includes RZ)	
Called	Average	Called	Success Rate
0	0.0	4	50%
2nd Down 6-1		2nd Down 7+	
Called	Average	Called	Average
0	0.0	0	0.0
Red Zone 10-0		Red Zone 10-20	
Called	Touchdown %	Called	Touchdown %
0	0%	0	0%

The 2018 Los Angeles Chargers Passing Index

Week	Quarter	Time	Down	ToGo	Location	Yards
Week 7 vs TEN	3	2:36	3	5	50	7
Week 11 vs DEN	2	11:16	3	8	LAC 15	27
Week 12 vs ARI	1	8:55	3	9	LAC 27	-10
Week 13 vs PIT	1	12:09	3	11	PIT 44	10

Most Often Paired With

- Backside Dig Combo
- Curl/Flat

Backside Spot – Dig

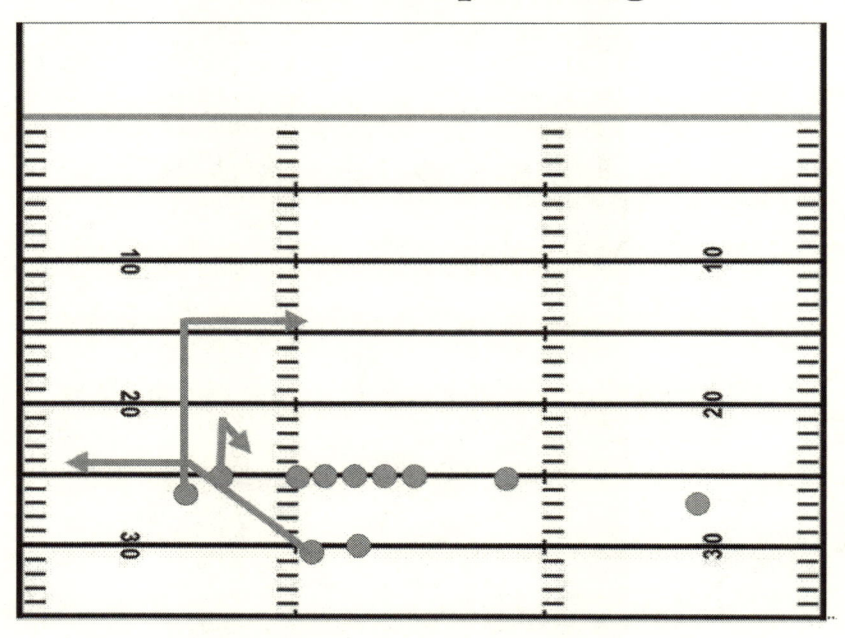

Average Yards per Play	4.5

1st Down	
Called	Average
3	-2.3
2nd Down 6-1	
Called	Average
0	0.0
Red Zone 10-0	
Called	Touchdown %
3	33%

Third Down (includes RZ)	
Called	Success Rate
8	38%
2nd Down 7+	
Called	Average
1	12.0
Red Zone 10-20	
Called	Touchdown %
2	50%

The 2018 Los Angeles Chargers Passing Index

Week	Quarter	Time	Down	ToGo	Location	Yards
Week 2 vs BUF	1	9:32	2	7	BUF 10	10
Week 3 vs LAR	2	8:19	3	10	LAC 1	3
Week 3 vs LAR	3	8:28	4	2	RAM 20	20
Week 4 vs SF	1	0:52	2	5	SFO 5	0
Week 4 vs SF	2	2:03	3	2	SFO 31	2
Week 5 vs OAK	1	5:41	3	4	LAC 37	19
Week 6 vs CLE	1	0:06	3	5	LAC 9	0
Week 10 vs OAK	3	3:05	3	2	LAC 43	0
Week 12 vs ARI	3	1:41	3	4	CRD 18	3
WC vs BAL	1	11:08	3	2	LAC 31	-1
Week 17 vs DEN	3	4:34	3	3	DEN 9	6
WC vs BAL	2	8:51	1	10	LAC 41	3
WC vs BAL	2	6:42	2	16	LAC 49	12
WC vs BAL	2	0:25	1	10	RAV 35	0
DIV vs NE	2	1:43	1	10	LAC 25	-10

Most Often Paired With
- Smash (Whip)
- Weakside Option
- Deep Hitch - Seam

Backside Dig – Drag – HB Burst

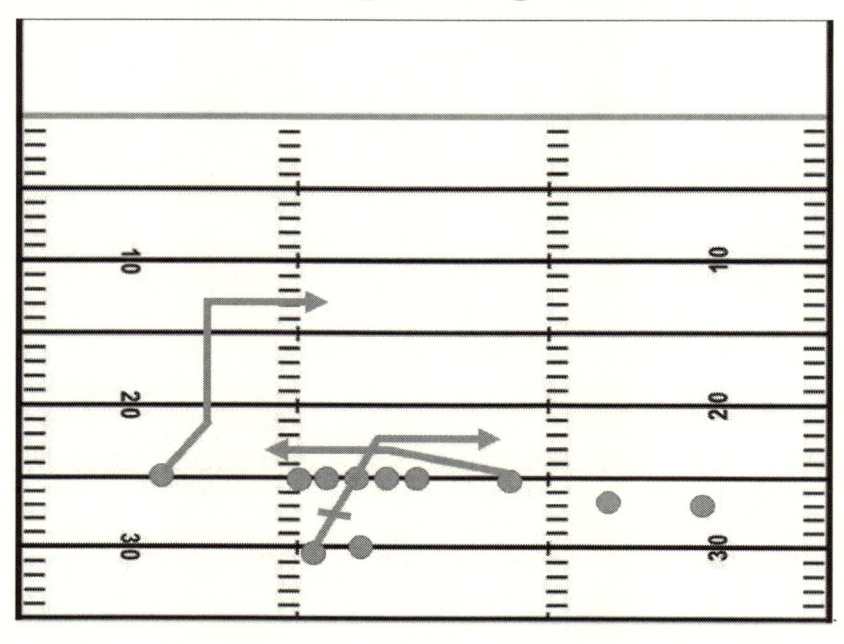

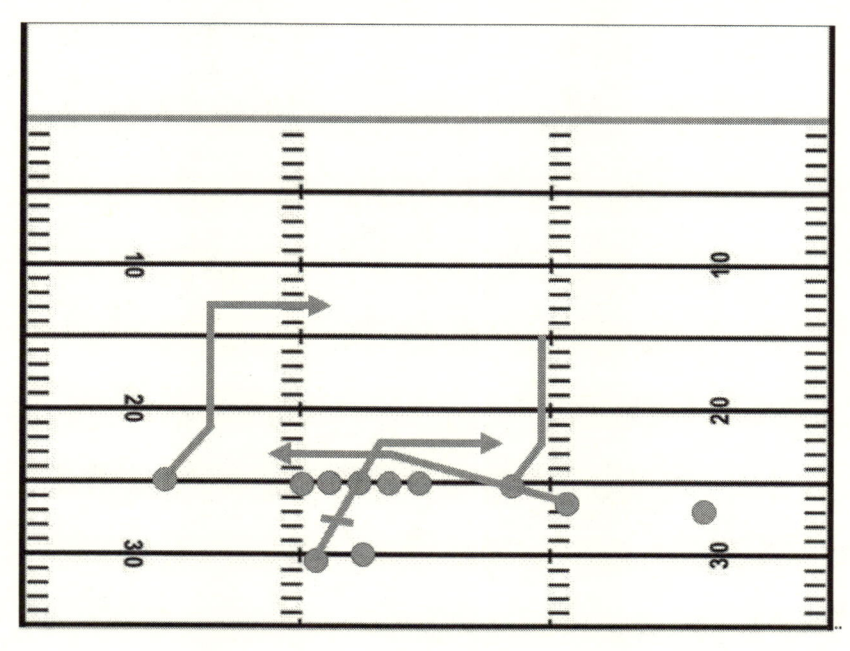

The 2018 Los Angeles Chargers Passing Index

Average Yards per Play	4.2

1st Down		Third Down (includes RZ)	
Called	Average	Called	Success Rate
2	10.0	4	0%

2nd Down 6-1		2nd Down 7+	
Called	Average	Called	Average
2	-2.5	5	6.8

Red Zone 10-0		Red Zone 10-20	
Called	Touchdown %	Called	Touchdown %
0	0%	1	0%

Week	Quarter	Time	Down	ToGo	Location	Yards
Week 5 vs OAK	1	11:52	3	5	RAI 25	-6
Week 5 vs OAK	2	12:34	2	14	LAC 20	9
Week 6 vs CLE	3	8:06	1	25	LAC 20	20
Week 7 vs TEN	3	7:32	2	4	LAC 43	-8
Week 7 vs TEN	3	6:45	3	12	LAC 35	11
Week 12 vs ARI	3	11:47	2	20	LAC 45	14
Week 12 vs ARI	3	6:04	1	10	LAC 27	0
Week 14 vs CIN	1	2:55	2	17	LAC 39	16
Week 15 vs KC	4	1:59	2	10	KAN 39	3
Week 16 vs BAL	1	12:06	2	5	LAC 30	3
Week 16 vs BAL	2	0:50	3	10	RAV 20	0
Week 16 vs BAL	3	10:34	2	19	LAC 28	-8
Week 17 vs DEN	1	8:30	3	8	DEN 49	0

Most Often Paired With:

- Deep Hitch – Seam
- Dusty

Trips Dig – (high-low #3)

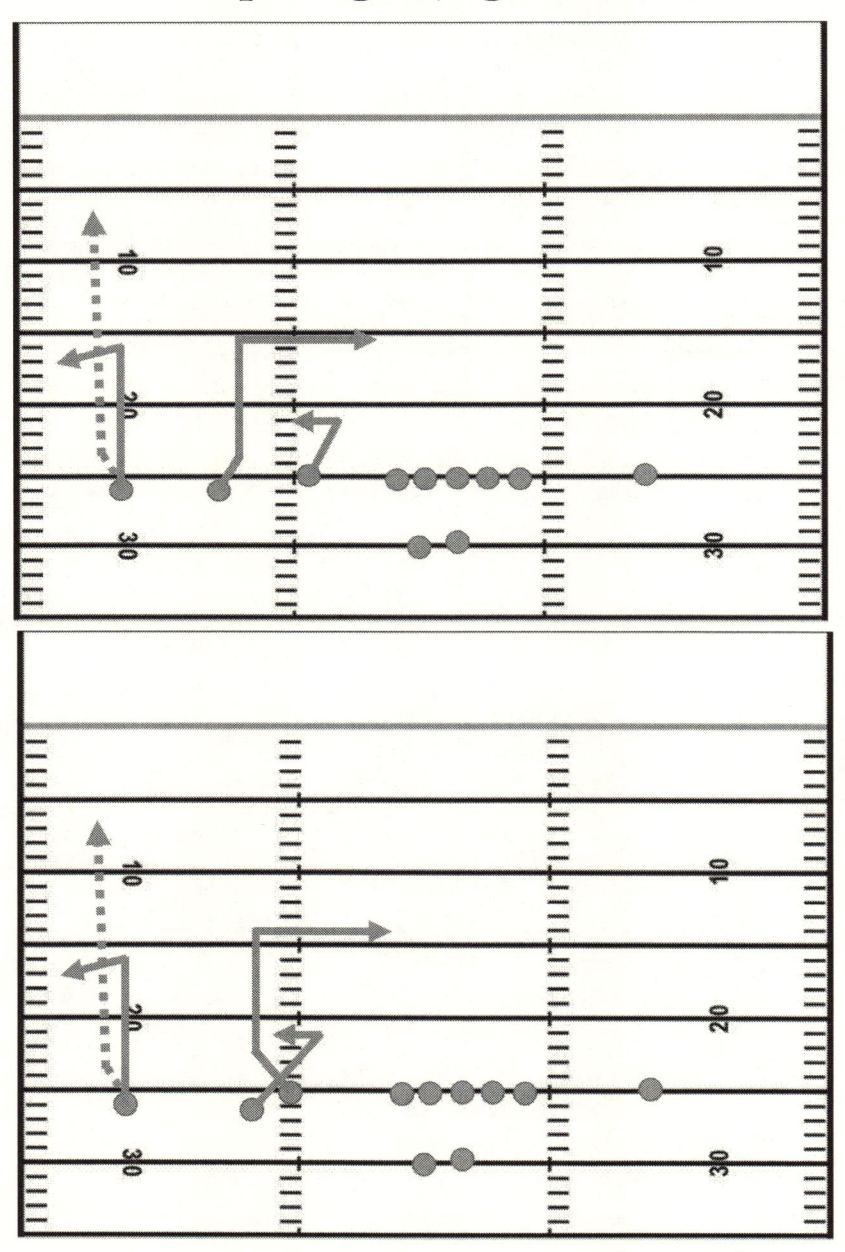

The 2018 Los Angeles Chargers Passing Index

Average Yards per Play	7.1

1st Down		Third Down (includes RZ)	
Called	Average	Called	Success Rate
3	11.0	3	67%
2nd Down 6-1		2nd Down 7+	
Called	Average	Called	Average
2	11.5	4	4.3
Red Zone 10-0		Red Zone 10-20	
Called	Touchdown %	Called	Touchdown %
1	100%	1	0%

Week	Quarter	Time	Down	ToGo	Location	Yards
Week 1 vs KC	1	11:44	2	7	LAC 40	8
Week 3 vs LAR	3	1:05	2	10	LAC 49	16
Week 4 vs SF	1	0:48	3	5	SFO 5	5
Week 5 vs OAK	3	12:33	2	6	LAC 30	16
Week 7 vs TEN	1	1:54	3	7	OTI 11	0
Week 13 vs PIT	2	7:41	2	13	LAC 32	0
Week 14 vs CIN	1	13:42	1	10	LAC 48	19
Week 15 vs KC	1	6:58	2	10	KAN 45	-7
Week 16 vs BAL	2	2:14	2	2	LAC 32	7
Week 16 vs BAL	4	1:31	3	10	RAV 43	TO
Week 17 vs DEN	1	5:57	1	10	LAC 28	14
Week 17 vs DEN	3	8:18	1	10	LAC 35	0

Most Often Paired With:

- Weakside Option Route
- Smash

"Swirl" Route

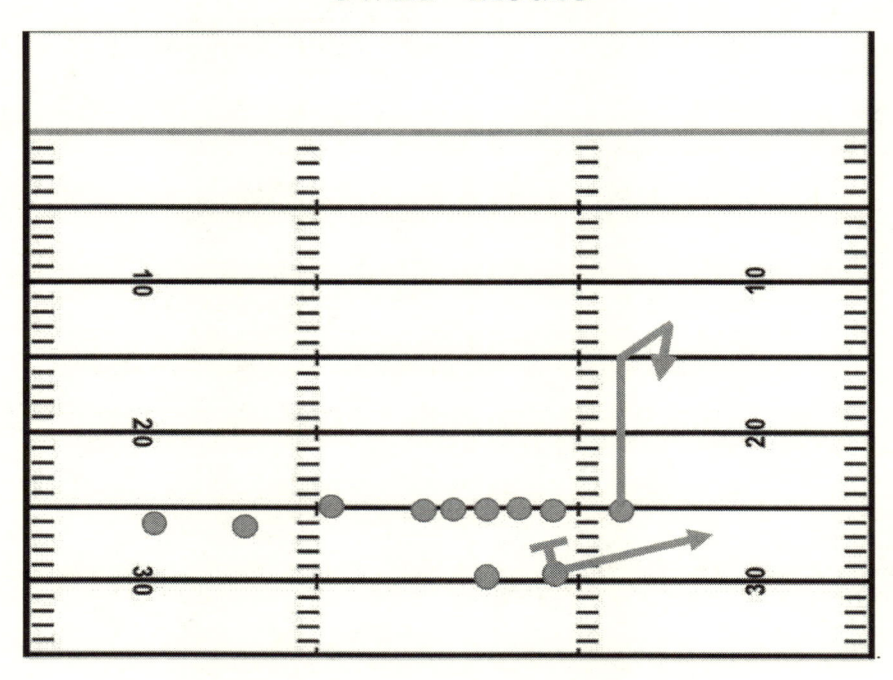

Average Yards per Play	12.1

1st Down		Third Down (includes RZ)	
Called	Average	Called	Success Rate
4	20.5	6	50%
2nd Down 6-1		2nd Down 7+	
Called	Average	Called	Average
1	16.0	1	30.0
Red Zone 10-0		Red Zone 10-20	
Called	Touchdown %	Called	Touchdown %
2	50%	0	0%

The 2018 Los Angeles Chargers Passing Index

Week	Quarter	Time	Down	ToGo	Location	Yards
Week 3 vs LAR	2	15:00	3	6	LAC 29	0
Week 5 vs OAK	2	3:24	1	17	LAC 45	11
Week 5 vs OAK	3	12:33	2	6	LAC 30	16
Week 5 vs OAK	3	9:51	3	11	RAI 37	16
Week 5 vs OAK	4	11:16	3	11	RAI 31	12
Week 6 vs CLE	3	12:47	3	10	LAC 44	-12
Week 7 vs TEN	1	6:55	1	10	LAC 22	11
Week 9 vs SEA	2	1:17	2	10	SEA 30	30
Week 9 vs SEA	3	0:04	3	8	LAC 28	0
Week 12 vs ARI	3	8:52	2	5	CRD 9	5
Week 12 vs ARI	3	8:09	1	4	CRD 4	4
Week 13 vs PIT	1	1:12	1	10	PIT 46	46
Week 15 vs KC	2	8:03	1	10	LAC 5	14
WC vs BAL	2	12:40	3	6	LAC 14	17

Most Often Paired With

- Hank

Post - Wheel

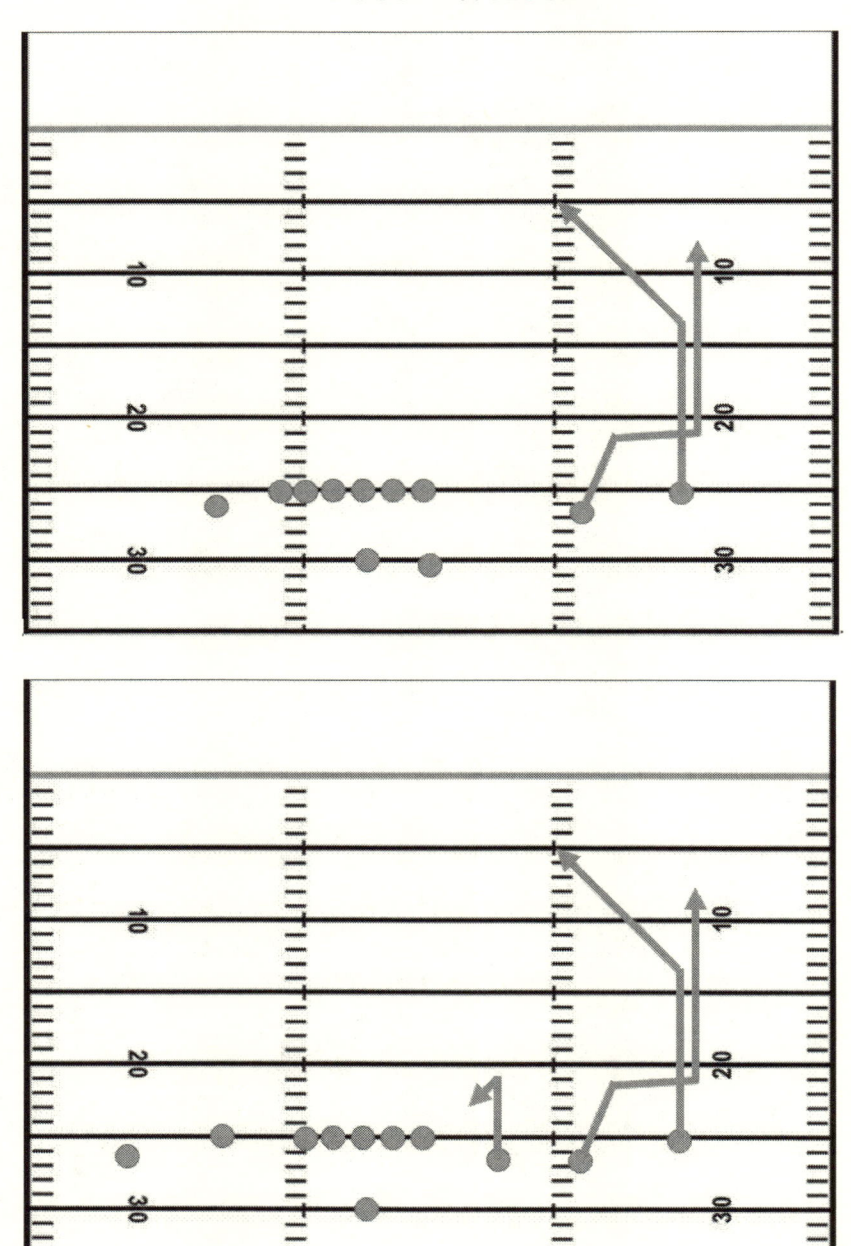

The 2018 Los Angeles Chargers Passing Index

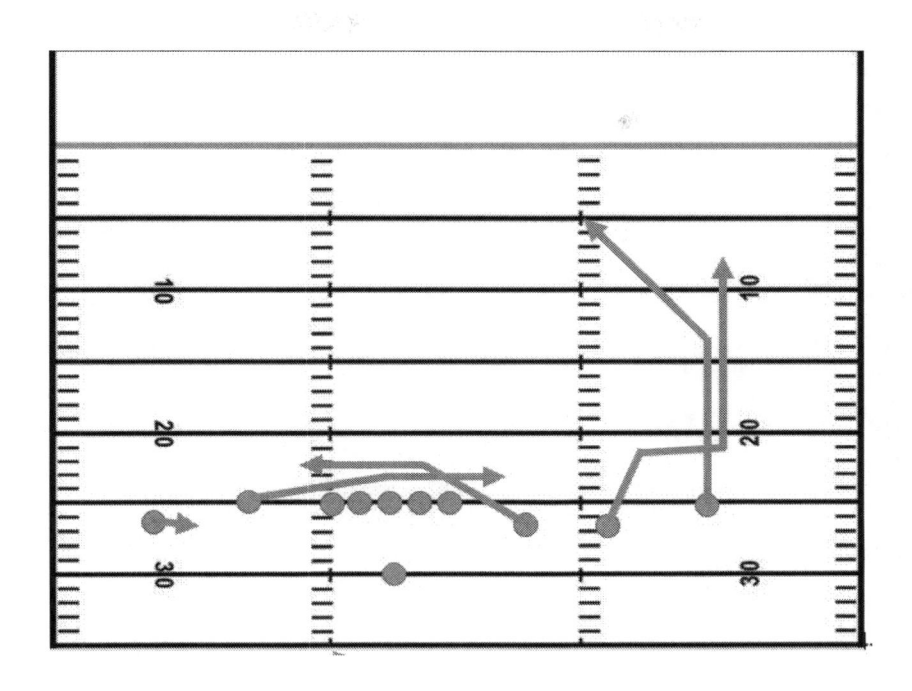

Average Yards per Play	12.5

1st Down		Third Down (includes RZ)	
Called	Average	Called	Success Rate
5	20.4	0	0%
2nd Down 6-1		2nd Down 7+	
Called	Average	Called	Average
1	9.0	4	9.5
Red Zone 10-0		Red Zone 10-20	
Called	Touchdown %	Called	Touchdown %
0	0%	2	50%

Week	Quarter	Time	Down	ToGo	Location	Yards
Week 2 vs BUF	2	7:15	2	7	LAC 33	8
DIV vs NE	3	3:34	2	13	NWE 20	0
Week 12 vs ARI	1	4:15	1	10	LAC 42	27
Week 12 vs ARI	1	3:18	2	6	CRD 27	9
Week 2 vs BUF	1	10:53	1	10	BUF 38	25
Week 1 vs KC	4	6:36	1	10	KAN 35	0
Week 13 vs PIT	1	1:58	2	9	LAC 40	14
Week 11 vs DEN	3	5:10	2	7	LAC 48	16
Week 7 vs TEN	1	1:59	2	7	OTI 11	0
Week 11 vs DEN	2	11:21	2	8	LAC 15	0
Week 1 vs KC	2	7:54	2	10	KAN 13	13
Week 13 vs PIT	1	1:12	1	10	PIT 46	46
Week 2 vs BUF	3	11:06	1	10	LAC 25	4

The 2018 Los Angeles Chargers Passing Index

Post Wheel – Drive HB Swing Strong

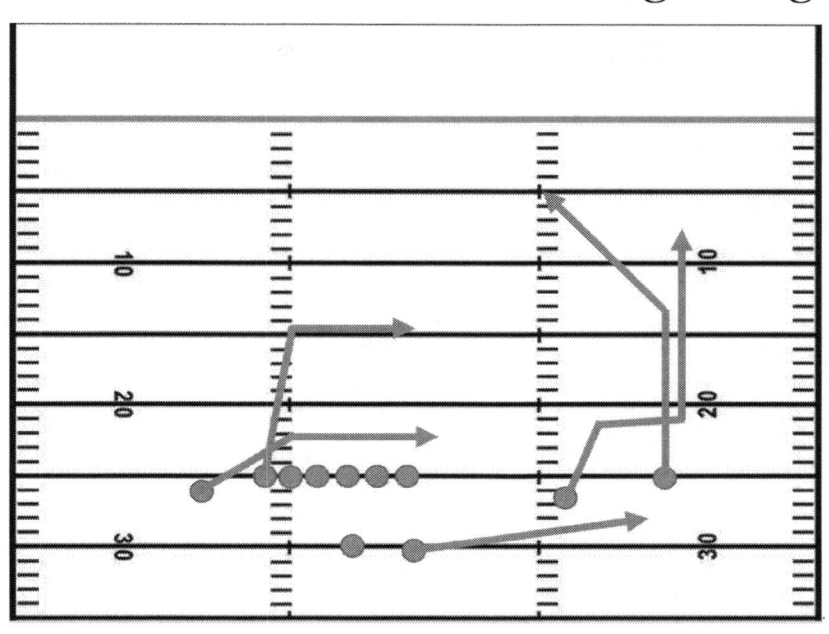

Average Yards per Play	16.3

1st Down	
Called	Average
6	16.3

Third Down (includes RZ)	
Called	Success Rate
0	0%

2nd Down 6-1	
Called	Average
0	0.0

2nd Down 7+	
Called	Average
0	0.0

Red Zone 10-0	
Called	Touchdown %
0	0%

Red Zone 10-20	
Called	Touchdown %
0	0%

Week	Quarter	Time	Down	ToGo	Location	Yards
Week 2 vs BUF	1	7:42	1	10	LAC 39	10
Week 2 vs BUF	4	12:39	1	10	LAC 20	18
Week 3 vs LAR	3	3:13	1	10	LAC 34	9
Week 13 vs PIT	2	5:13	1	10	LAC 17	6
Week 14 vs CIN	1	2:04	1	10	CIN 42	17
Week 15 vs KC	1	0:43	1	10	LAC 25	38

Flood (3 man)

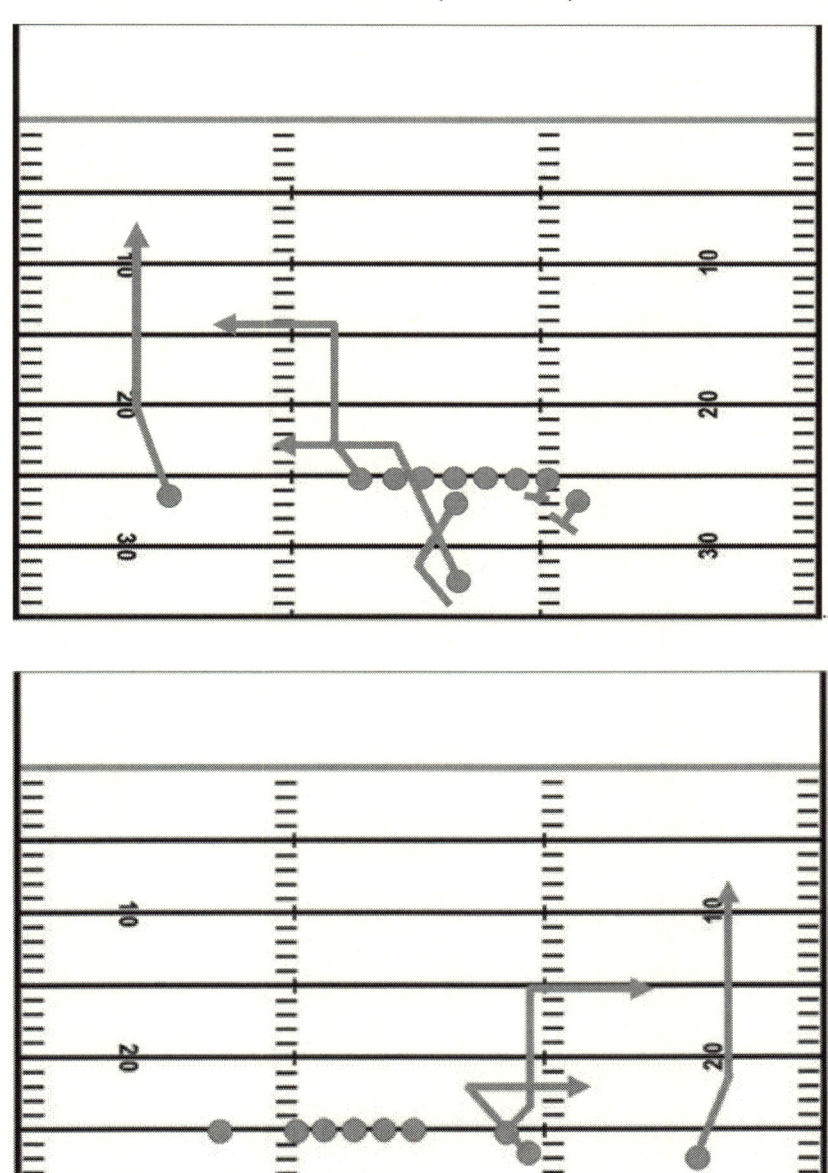

Bobby Peters

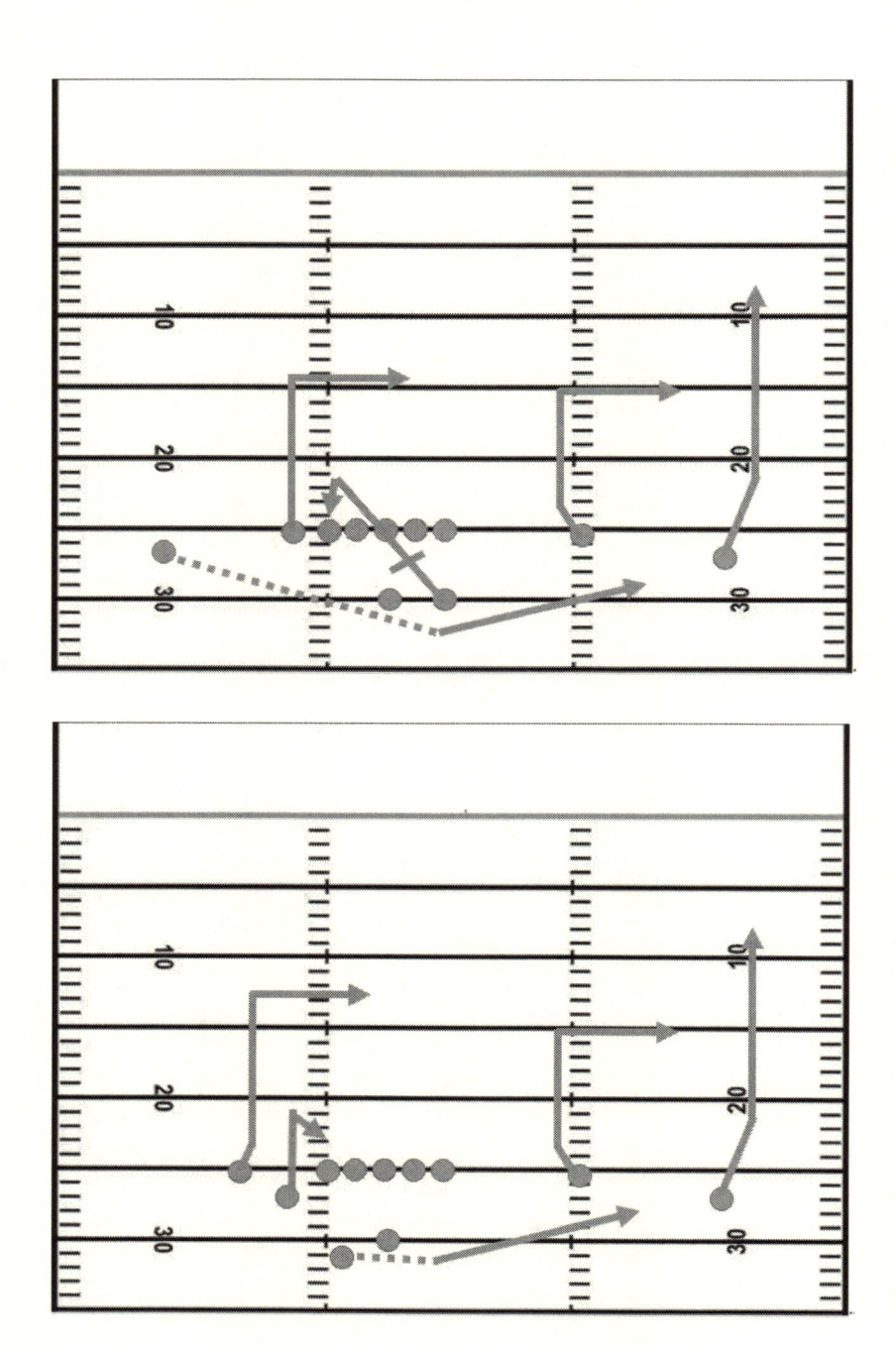

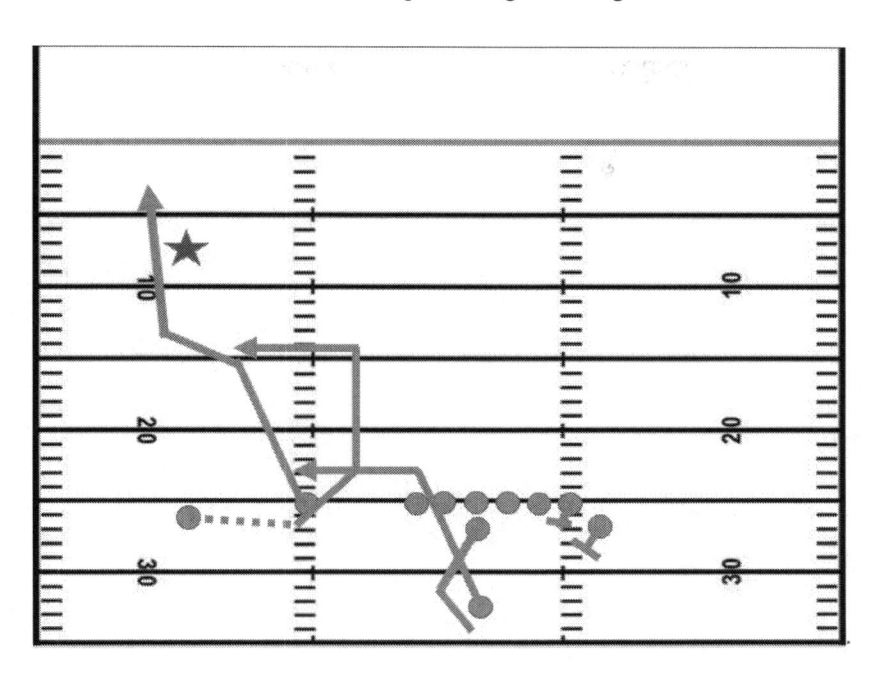

The 2018 Los Angeles Chargers Passing Index

Average Yards per Play	8.8

1st Down	
Called	Average
6	7.7

Third Down (includes RZ)	
Called	Success Rate
5	60%

2nd Down 6-1	
Called	Average
0	0.0

2nd Down 7+	
Called	Average
2	8.5

Red Zone 10-0	
Called	Touchdown %
0	0%

Red Zone 10-20	
Called	Touchdown %
0	0%

Week	Quarter	Time	Down	ToGo	Location	Yards
Week 1 vs KC	1	10:09	2	8	KAN 31	0
Week 1 vs KC	1	3:18	1	10	KAN 42	13
Week 1 vs KC	3	4:21	3	4	KAN 26	TO
Week 4 vs SF	1	11:32	1	10	LAC 37	2
Week 9 vs SEA	3	9:32	1	10	SEA 43	13
Week 9 vs SEA	3	2:26	1	10	LAC 5	0
Week 11 vs DEN	2	3:25	3	4	DEN 33	29
Week 12 vs ARI	2	5:07	1	20	CRD 29	24
Week 15 vs KC	3	10:52	2	8	LAC 26	17
Week 17 vs DEN	1	8:30	3	8	DEN 49	0
WC vs BAL	1	1:56	3	7	RAV 39	4
WC vs BAL	2	7:27	1	10	RAV 45	-6
WC vs BAL	2	5:57	3	4	RAV 39	9

Most Often Paired With:

- Backside Dig Combos
- Max Protection

Second Diagram: Wild Card Game (two times)

Third Diagram: Week 4

Fourth Diagram: Week 15 (completion to backside dig)

Fifth Diagram: Week 1 1Q 10:09

Flood (4 man & Seattle)

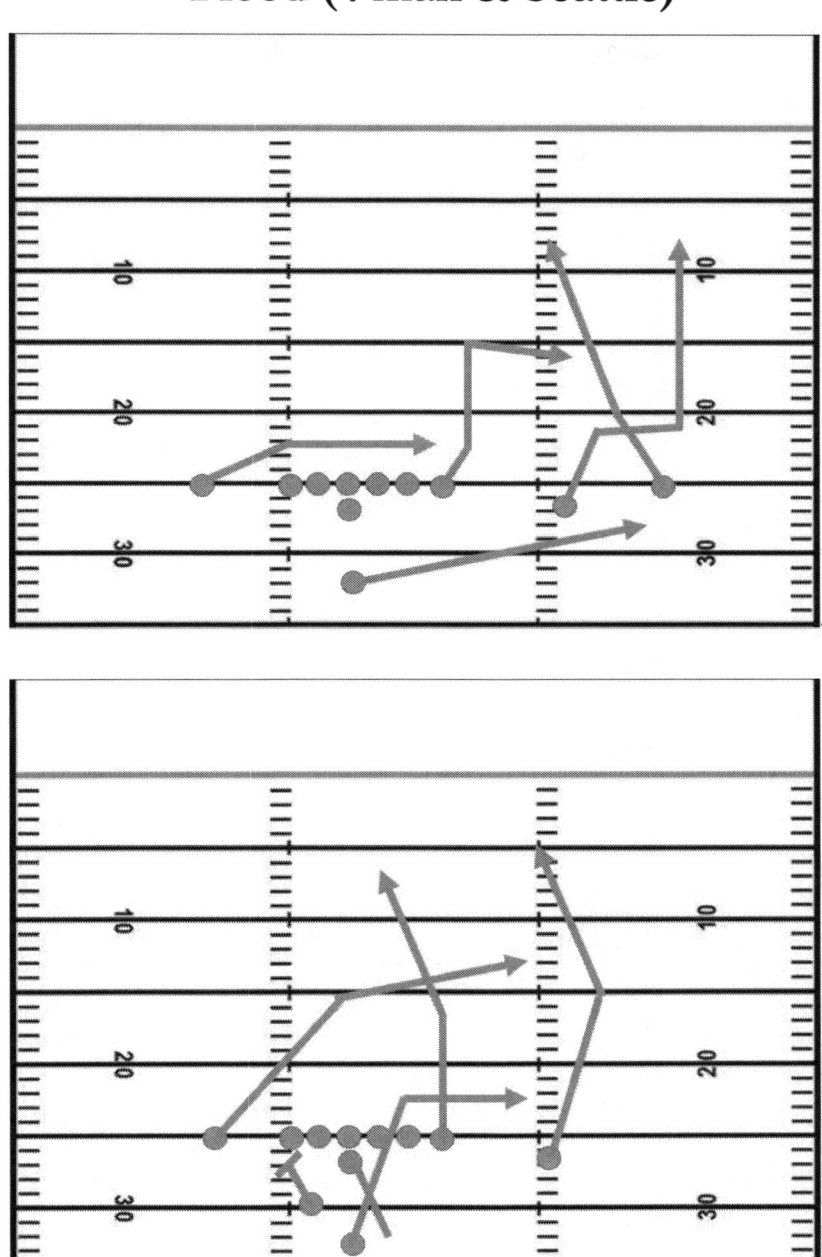

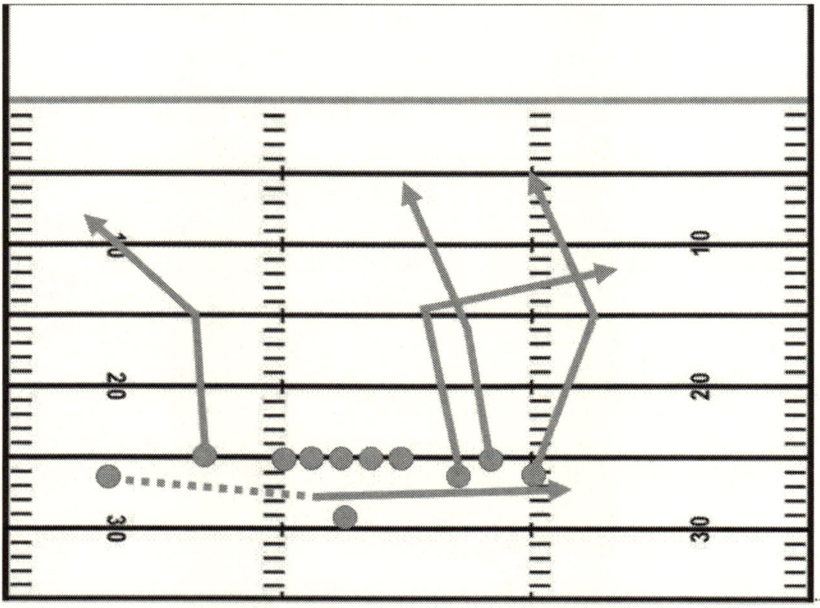
10
20
30
10
20
30

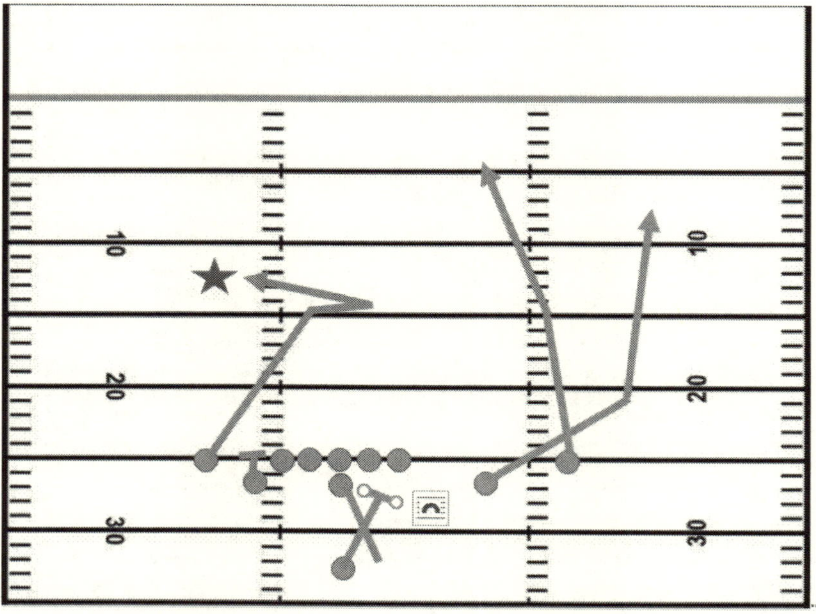
10
20
30
10
20
30

The 2018 Los Angeles Chargers Passing Index

Average Yards per Play	7.4

1st Down		Third Down (includes RZ)	
Called	Average	Called	Success Rate
4	8.3	0	0%
2nd Down 6-1		2nd Down 7+	
Called	Average	Called	Average
1	10.0	2	4.5
Red Zone 10-0		Red Zone 10-20	
Called	Touchdown %	Called	Touchdown %
0	0%	0	0%

Week	Quarter	Time	Down	ToGo	Location	Yards
Week 2 vs BUF	2	5:42	2	3	BUF 30	10
Week 3 vs LAR	1	0:51	1	10	LAC 25	1
Week 9 vs SEA	1	6:15	1	10	LAC 34	10
Week 9 vs SEA	3	10:54	1	10	LAC 15	22
Week 11 vs DEN	3	5:10	2	7	LAC 48	16
Week 12 vs ARI	1	10:14	1	10	LAC 26	0
Week 16 vs BAL	3	4:25	2	16	LAC 19	-7

First Diagram: Week 9 and Week 12

Second Diagram: Week 3

Third Diagram: Week 2

Fourth Diagram: Week 11

H Angle

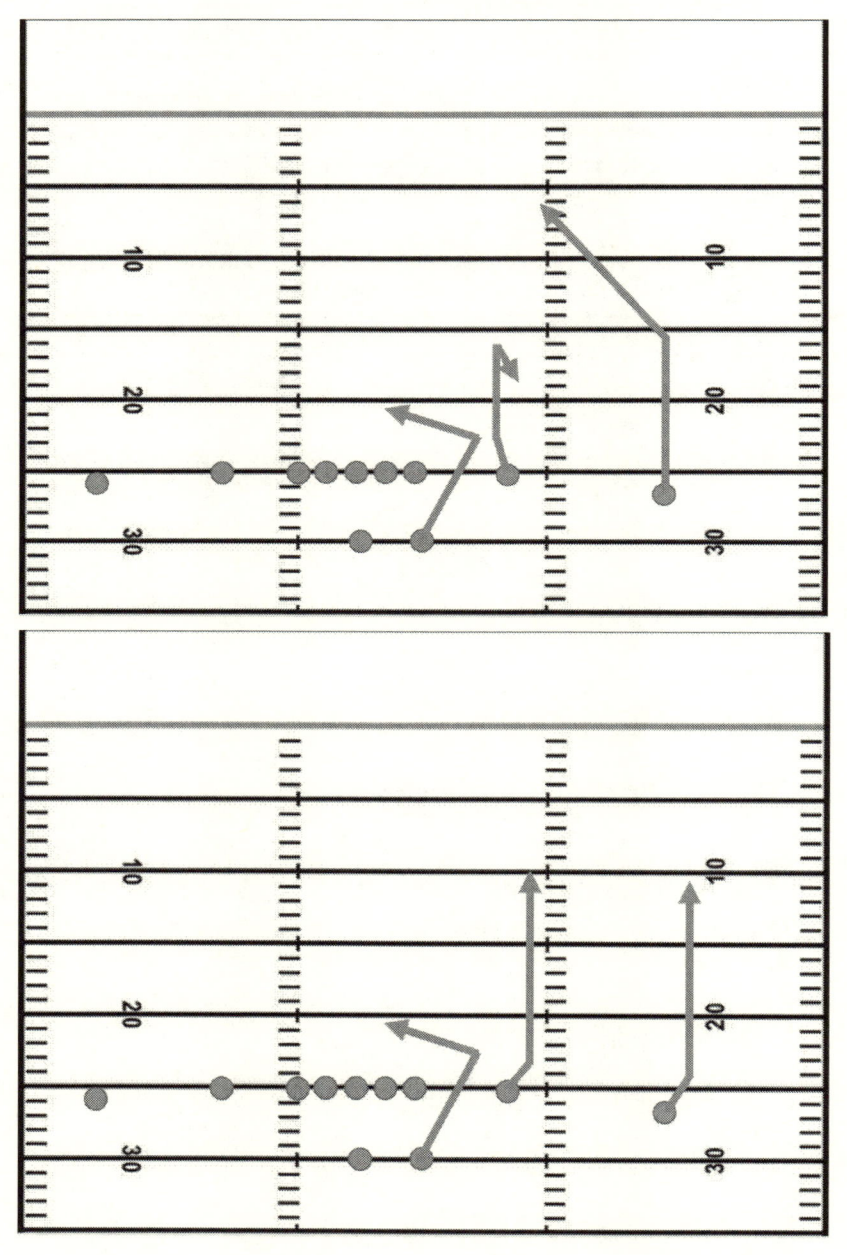

The 2018 Los Angeles Chargers Passing Index

Average Yards per Play	5.8

1st Down		Third Down (includes RZ)	
Called	Average	Called	Success Rate
0	0.0	0	0%

2nd Down 6-1		2nd Down 7+	
Called	Average	Called	Average
2	9.5	1	16.0

Red Zone 10-0		Red Zone 10-20	
Called	Touchdown %	Called	Touchdown %
0	0%	2	0%

Week	Quarter	Time	Down	ToGo	Location	Yards
Week 4 vs SF	3	11:29	1	10	SFO 12	0
Week 1 vs KC	4	2:56	2	10	LAC 14	16
Week 14 vs CIN	3	7:55	2	10	CIN 13	0
Week 12 vs ARI	2	1:26	2	2	LAC 28	9
Week 12 vs ARI	2	0:34	2	6	CRD 40	10
DIV vs NE	4	12:08	2	20	LAC 14	0

Play Action – Quick Slant

The 2018 Los Angeles Chargers Passing Index

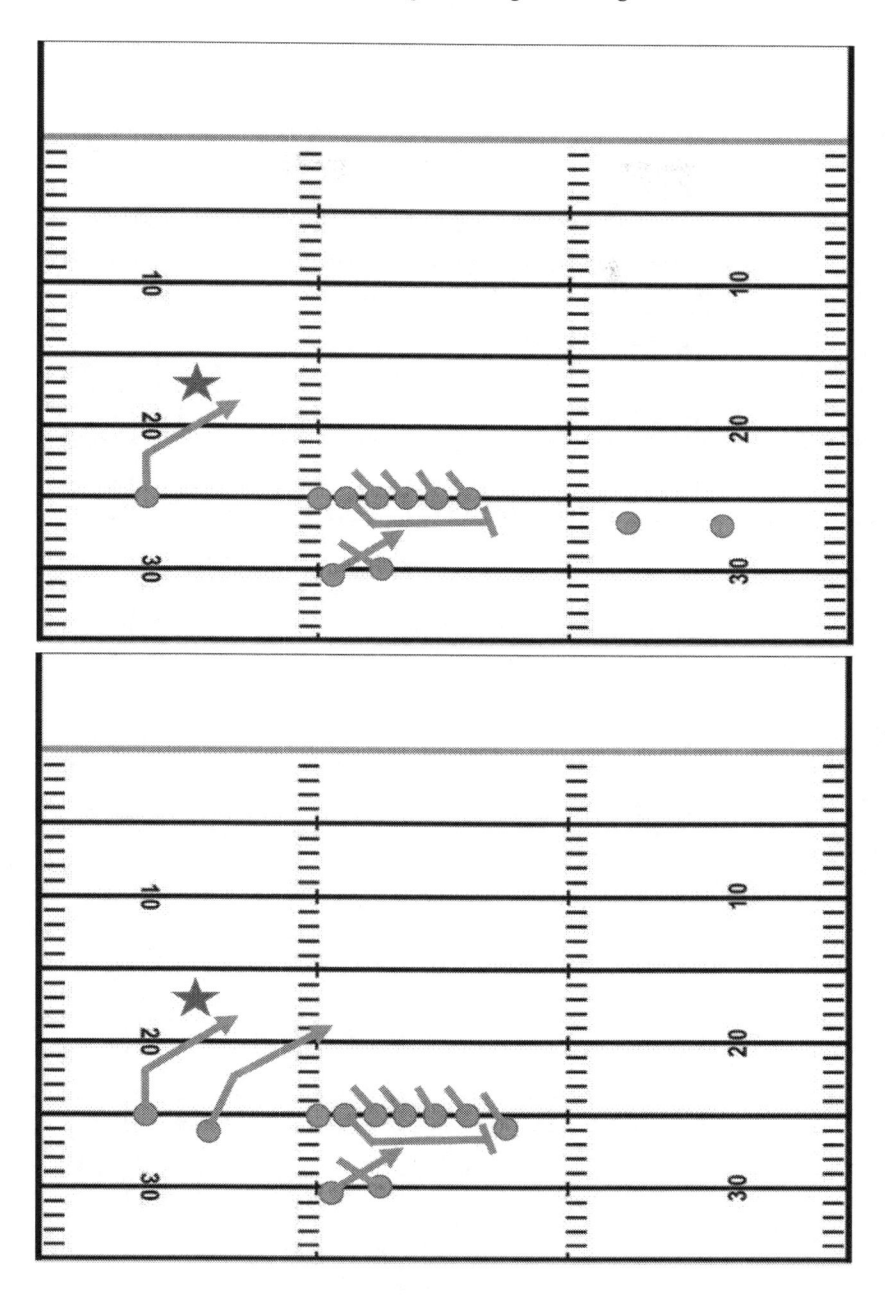

77

Average Yards per Play	3.0

1st Down		Third Down (includes RZ)	
Called	Average	Called	Success Rate
0	0.0	1	0%
2nd Down 6-1		2nd Down 7+	
Called	Average	Called	Average
0	0.0	3	4.7
Red Zone 10-0		Red Zone 10-20	
Called	Touchdown %	Called	Touchdown %
3	67%	1	0%

Week	Quarter	Time	Down	ToGo	Location	Yards
Week 1 vs KC	1	5:35	2	10	KAN 30	0
Week 1 vs KC	4	12:53	2	10	KAN 28	8
Week 1 vs KC	4	5:08	1	4	KAN 4	4
Week 14 vs CIN	2	15:00	1	5	CIN 5	0
Week 14 vs CIN	4	7:54	3	3	CIN 14	0
Week 17 vs DEN	3	3:51	1	3	DEN 3	3
WC vs BAL	2	13:27	2	12	LAC 8	6

Pin/Pull Slants RPO (Pass Thrown)

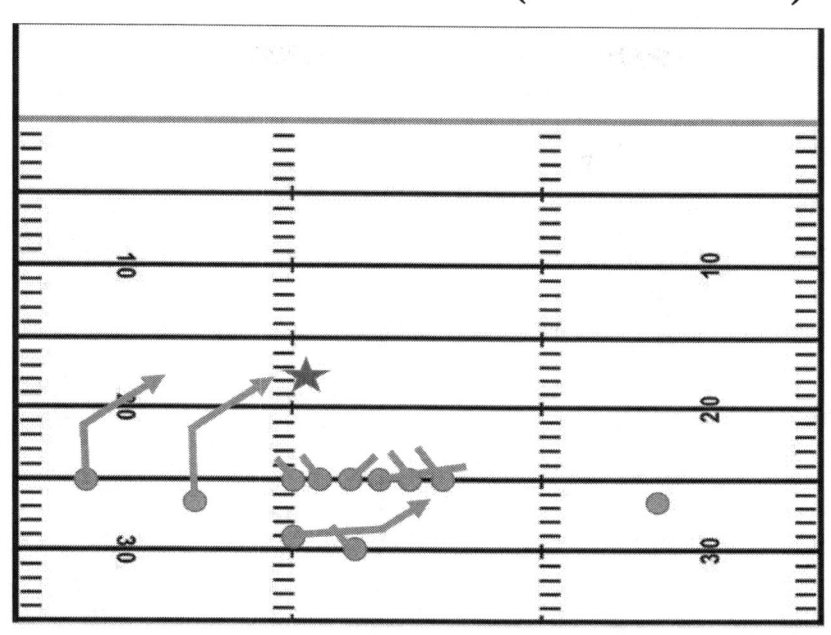

Average Yards per Play	9.5

1st Down	
Called	Average
5	11.4

Third Down (includes RZ)	
Called	Success Rate
0	0%

2nd Down 6-1	
Called	Average
0	0.0

2nd Down 7+	
Called	Average
1	0.0

Red Zone 10-0	
Called	Touchdown %
0	0%

Red Zone 10-20	
Called	Touchdown %
0	0%

Week	Quarter	Time	Down	ToGo	Location	Yards
Week 1 vs KC	1	15:00	1	10	LAC 25	8
Week 4 vs SF	2	4:59	1	10	LAC 25	16
Week 4 vs SF	4	12:39	1	10	LAC 25	8
Week 11 vs DEN	1	9:37	2	10	DEN 34	0
Week 15 vs KC	4	8:15	1	10	LAC 25	14
Week 17 vs DEN	2	12:05	1	10	LAC 11	11

Scissors – Backside Dig

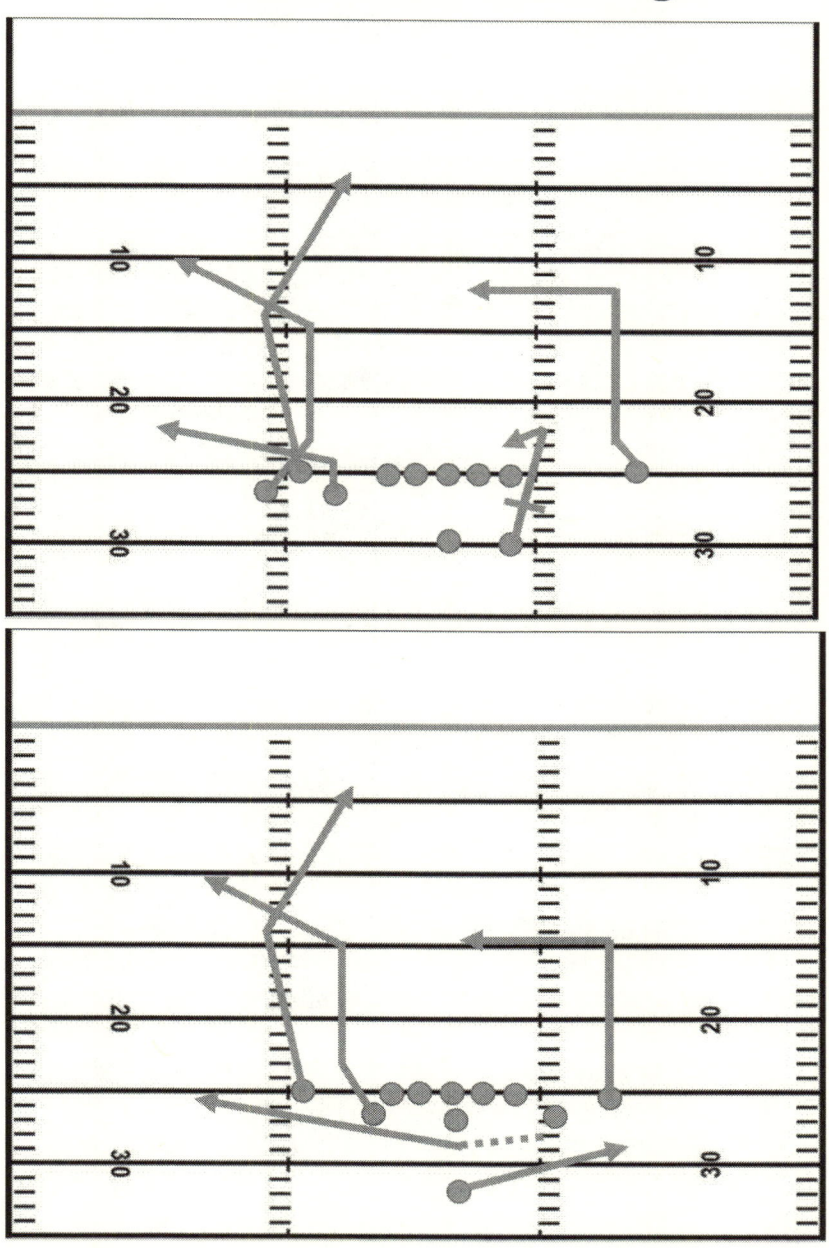

Bobby Peters

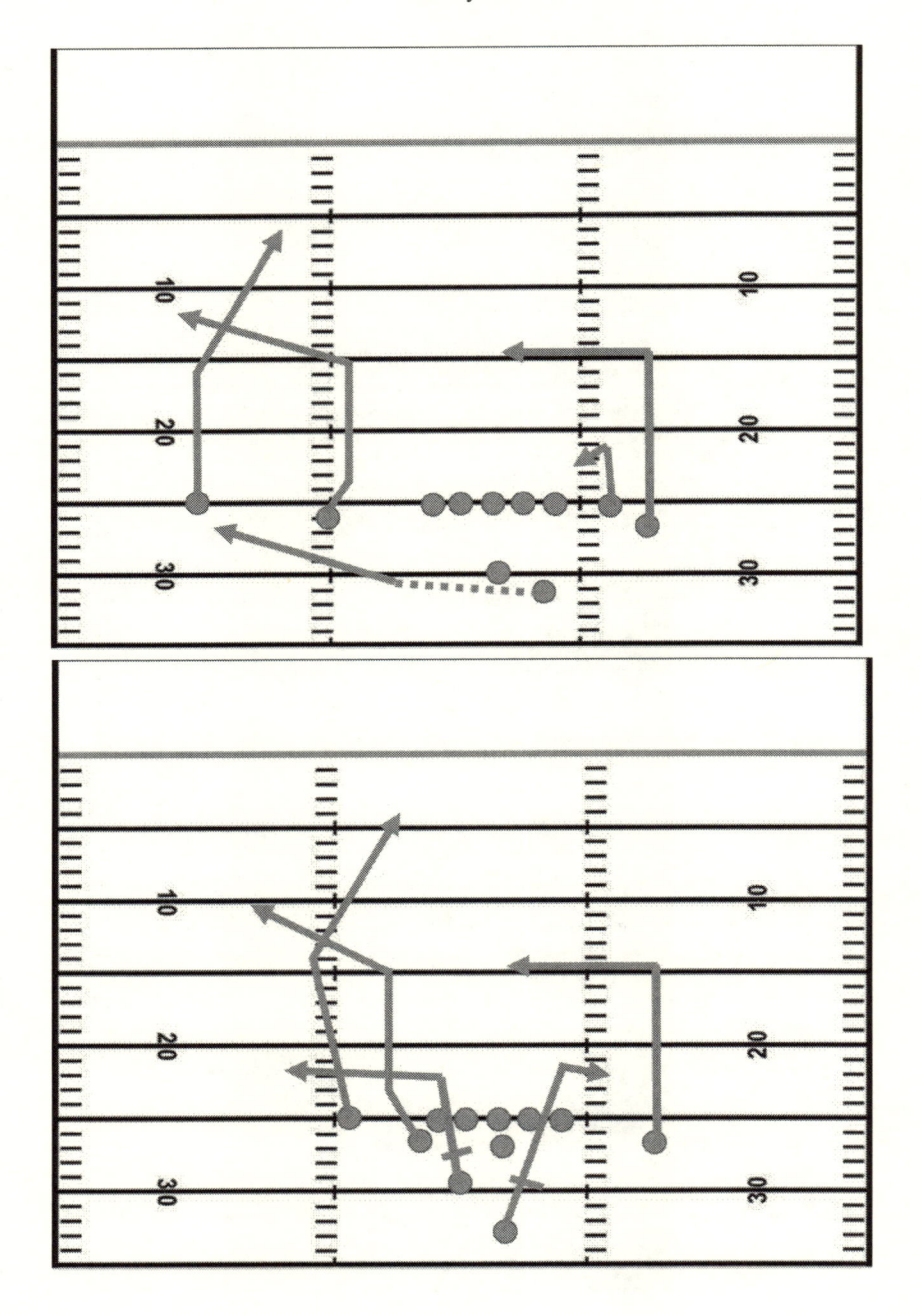

The 2018 Los Angeles Chargers Passing Index

Average Yards per Play	8.0

1st Down

Called	Average
4	6.0

Third Down (includes RZ)

Called	Success Rate
5	40%

2nd Down 6-1

Called	Average
0	0.0

2nd Down 7+

Called	Average
2	0.0

Red Zone 10-0

Called	Touchdown %
0	0%

Red Zone 10-20

Called	Touchdown %
0	0%

Week	Quarter	Time	Down	ToGo	Location	Yards
Week 1 vs KC	2	1:15	2	14	LAC 21	0
Week 1 vs KC	4	1:45	2	10	KAN 28	0
Week 5 vs OAK	2	8:38	1	10	50	0
Week 7 vs TEN	4	5:46	3	8	OTI 47	4
Week 11 vs DEN	1	9:32	3	10	DEN 34	14
Week 11 vs DEN	4	3:33	3	6	LAC 24	25
Week 14 vs CIN	1	15:00	1	10	LAC 25	5
Week 15 vs KC	1	6:29	3	17	LAC 48	8
Week 15 vs KC	4	7:47	1	10	LAC 39	0
Week 17 vs DEN	3	7:28	3	21	LAC 24	13
Week 17 vs DEN	4	14:49	1	10	LAC 9	19

Scissors – Corner (Max Protection)

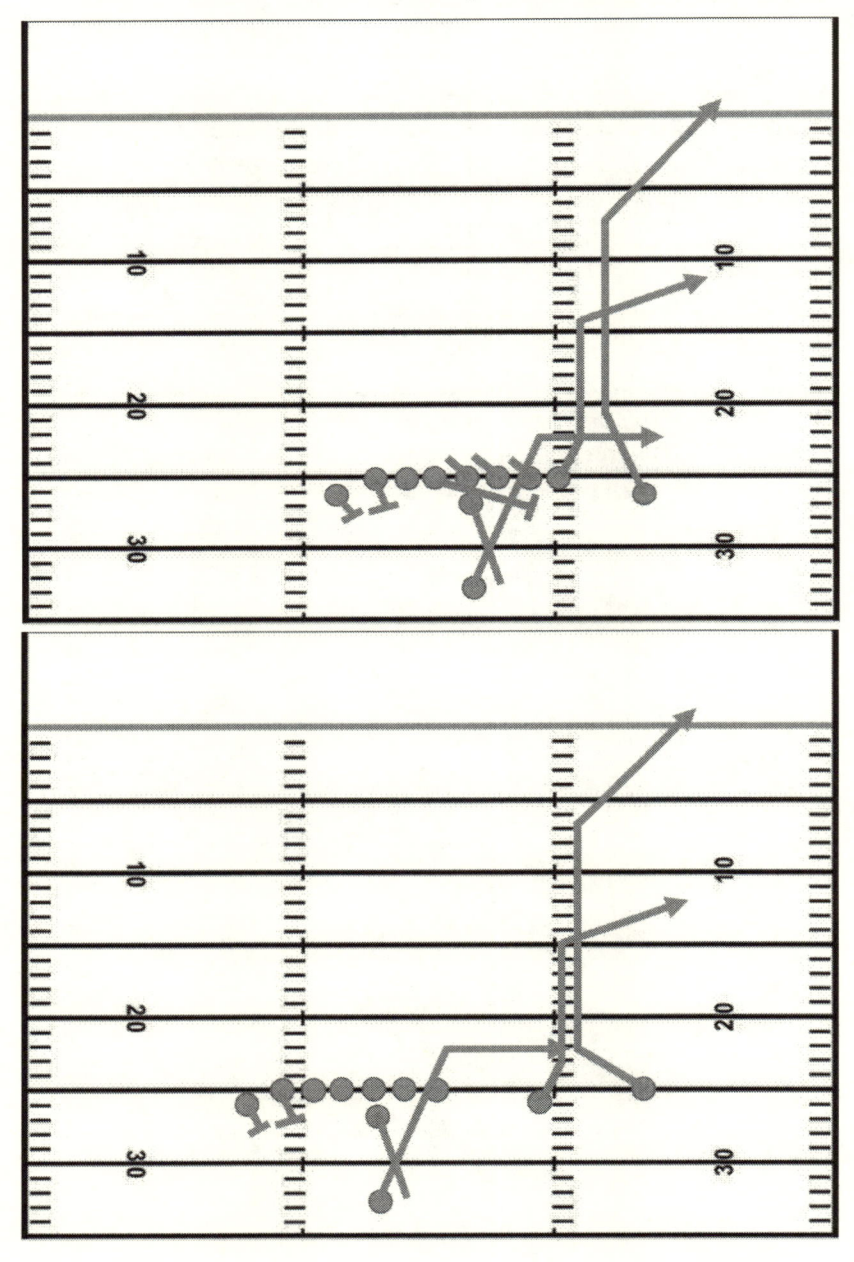

The 2018 Los Angeles Chargers Passing Index

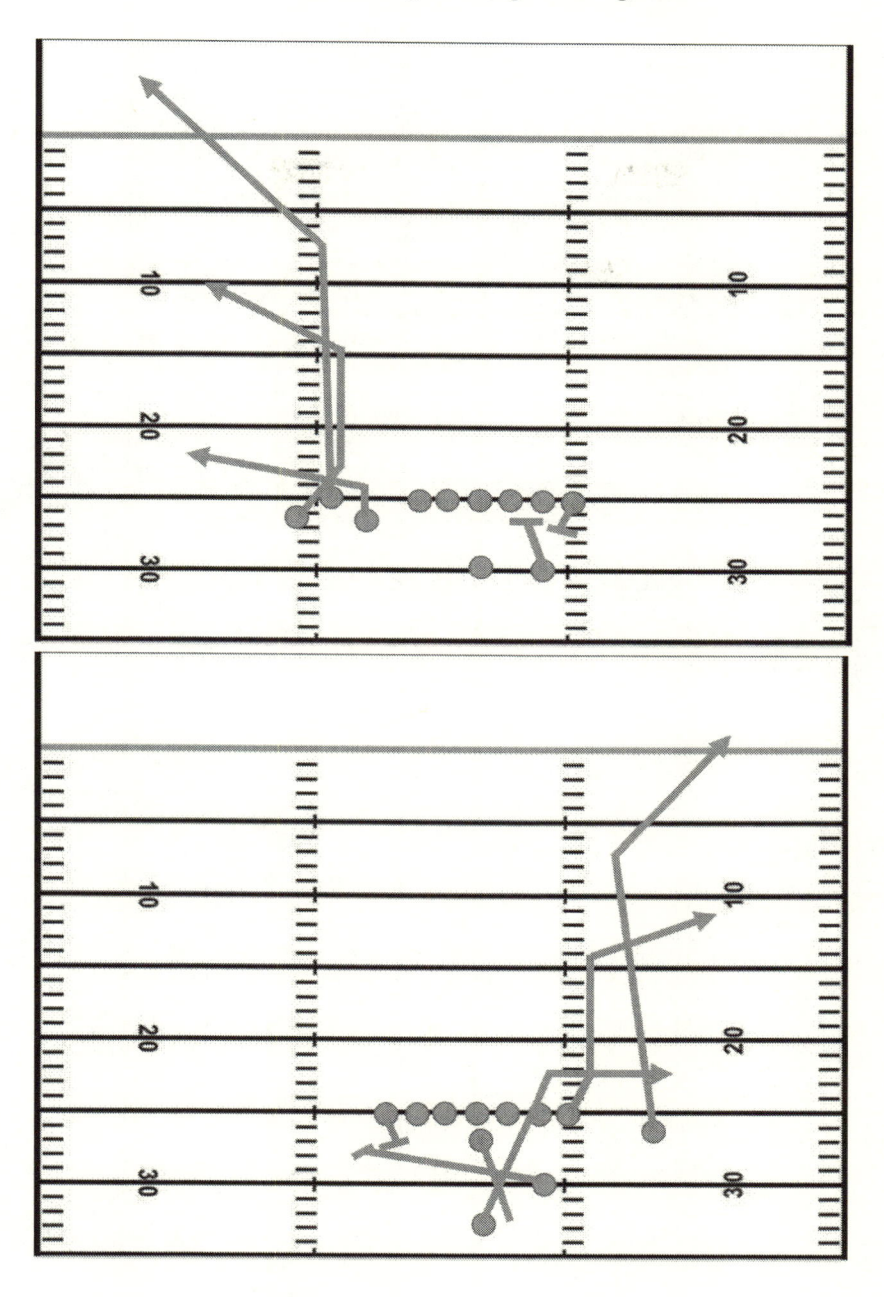

Average Yards per Play	15.7

1st Down	
Called	Average
4	12.0

Third Down (includes RZ)	
Called	Success Rate
0	0%

2nd Down 6-1	
Called	Average
2	31.0

2nd Down 7+	
Called	Average
1	0.0

Red Zone 10-0	
Called	Touchdown %
0	0%

Red Zone 10-20	
Called	Touchdown %
0	0%

Week	Quarter	Time	Down	ToGo	Location	Yards
Week 2 vs BUF	2	12:53	1	10	LAC 47	23
Week 4 vs SF	1	3:18	1	10	LAC 43	22
Week 7 vs TEN	3	13:52	2	3	LAC 45	55
Week 11 vs DEN	2	5:37	2	7	LAC 29	0
Week 11 vs DEN	2	0:05	1	10	LAC 39	-9
Week 11 vs DEN	3	6:36	2	6	LAC 38	7
Week 16 vs BAL	3	12:18	1	10	LAC 25	12

The 2018 Los Angeles Chargers Passing Index

Scissors – Corner

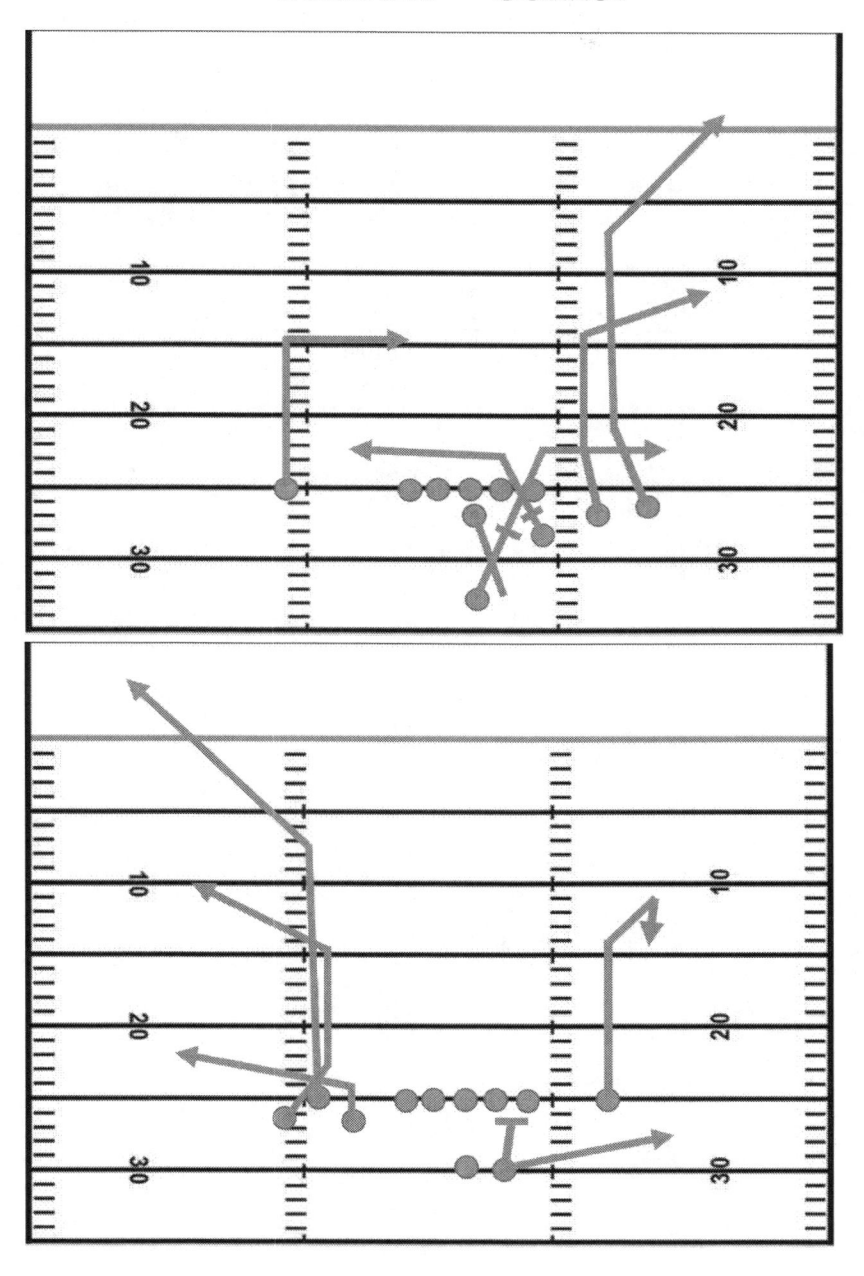

Average Yards per Play	10.2

1st Down		Third Down (includes RZ)	
Called	Average	Called	Success Rate
6	7.3	3	33%
2nd Down 6-1		**2nd Down 7+**	
Called	Average	Called	Average
1	31.0	5	9.8
Red Zone 10-0		**Red Zone 10-20**	
Called	Touchdown %	Called	Touchdown %
0	0%	0	0%

Week	Quarter	Time	Down	ToGo	Location	Yards
Week 4 vs SF	4	5:27	2	11	SFO 47	9
Week 5 vs OAK	3	9:51	3	11	RAI 37	16
Week 5 vs OAK	3	1:05	1	10	LAC 4	48
Week 10 vs OAK	2	3:02	2	5	LAC 14	31
Week 10 vs OAK	4	13:17	1	10	LAC 38	0
Week 10 vs OAK	4	13:13	2	10	LAC 38	11
Week 11 vs DEN	1	1:22	3	21	DEN 40	13
Week 12 vs ARI	2	9:40	1	10	LAC 36	-7
Week 13 vs PIT	2	7:37	3	13	LAC 32	0
Week 14 vs CIN	1	5:43	2	8	LAC 27	7
Week 15 vs KC	1	8:22	2	7	LAC 33	22
Week 15 vs KC	2	2:00	1	10	KAN 22	-5
Week 16 vs BAL	2	2:43	1	10	LAC 24	8
Week 17 vs DEN	2	10:52	1	10	LAC 35	0
Week 17 vs DEN	2	10:46	2	10	LAC 35	0

Slot Scissors

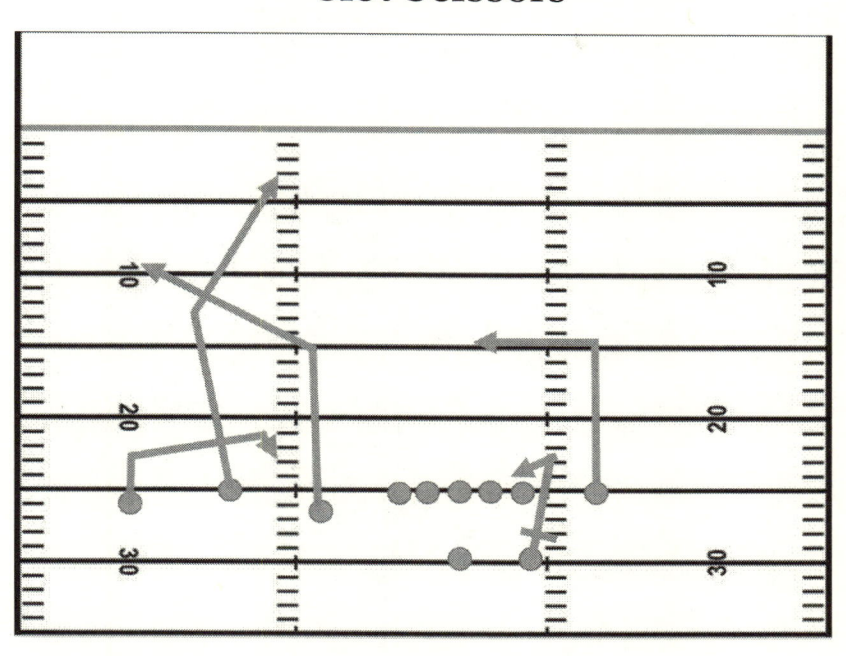

Average Yards per Play — 7.9

1st Down	
Called	Average
5	8.8

Third Down (includes RZ)	
Called	Success Rate
3	0%

2nd Down 6-1	
Called	Average
1	7.0

2nd Down 7+	
Called	Average
3	9.7

Red Zone 10-0	
Called	Touchdown %
0	0%

Red Zone 10-20	
Called	Touchdown %
1	0%

Week	Quarter	Time	Down	ToGo	Location	Yards
Week 1 vs KC	2	11:51	2	10	LAC 26	15
Week 1 vs KC	4	8:07	1	10	LAC 39	9
Week 3 vs LAR	4	5:28	3	10	RAM 22	3
Week 3 vs LAR	4	4:41	4	7	RAM 19	6
Week 6 vs CLE	2	1:42	2	10	CLE 33	4
Week 11 vs DEN	2	0:19	1	10	LAC 19	0
Week 15 vs KC	4	5:50	2	10	KAN 23	10
Week 15 vs KC	4	2:33	1	20	LAC 30	31
Week 16 vs BAL	4	2:19	2	2	LAC 33	7
WC vs BAL	2	10:32	3	2	LAC 39	0
WC vs BAL	2	0:45	1	10	LAC 40	0
WC vs BAL	4	9:19	3	10	RAV 29	0
DIV vs NE	4	9:39	1	10	LAC 20	29
DIV vs NE	4	5:04	1	10	LAC 2	0
Week 12 vs ARI	2	0:52	1	10	CRD 44	4

Four Verticals

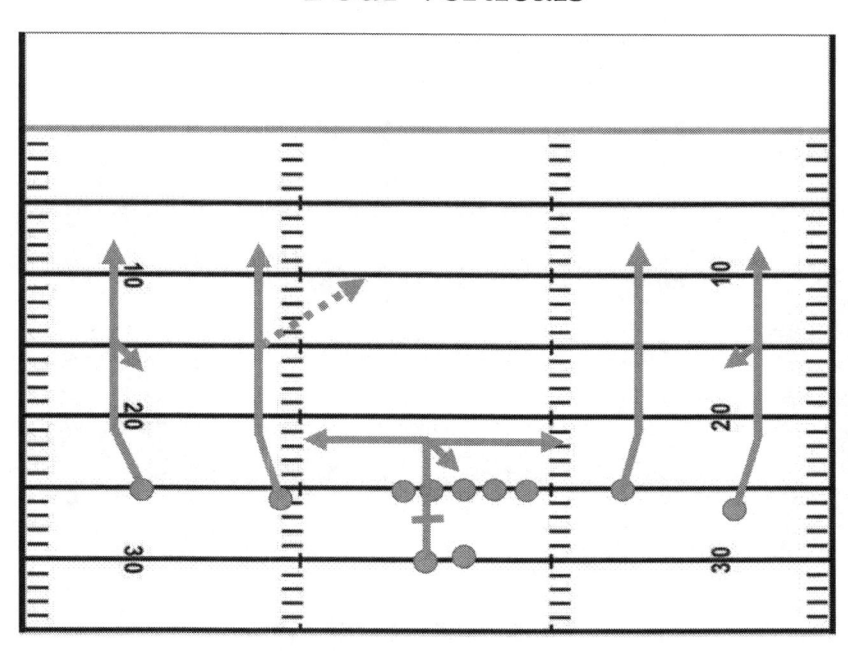

Average Yards per Play	7.1

1st Down	
Called	Average
3	15.3

Third Down (includes RZ)	
Called	Success Rate
7	0%

2nd Down 6-1	
Called	Average
0	0.0

2nd Down 7+	
Called	Average
2	6.5

Red Zone 10-0	
Called	Touchdown %
0	0%

Red Zone 10-20	
Called	Touchdown %
2	0%

Week	Quarter	Time	Down	ToGo	Location	Yards
Week 1 vs KC	4	2:29	1	10	LAC 30	13
Week 1 vs KC	4	2:03	1	10	LAC 43	17
Week 4 vs SF	1	13:20	2	7	LAC 28	0
Week 4 vs SF	3	11:29	1	10	SFO 12	0
Week 9 vs SEA	4	9:54	2	7	LAC 29	13
Week 13 vs PIT	1	7:53	3	19	LAC 12	0
Week 13 vs PIT	2	1:51	3	10	LAC 39	0
Week 14 vs CIN	2	10:42	3	12	LAC 5	0
Week 14 vs CIN	3	7:55	2	10	CIN 13	0
Week 15 vs KC	3	1:24	3	10	LAC 34	0
Week 15 vs KC	4	6:28	1	10	KAN 39	16
Week 15 vs KC	4	1:11	4	7	KAN 36	26
Week 16 vs BAL	3	9:50	3	27	LAC 20	10
Week 16 vs BAL	3	3:38	3	23	LAC 12	9
WC vs BAL	4	1:41	3	16	LAC 16	9
DIV vs NE	4	12:08	2	20	LAC 14	0

Verticals – Drag

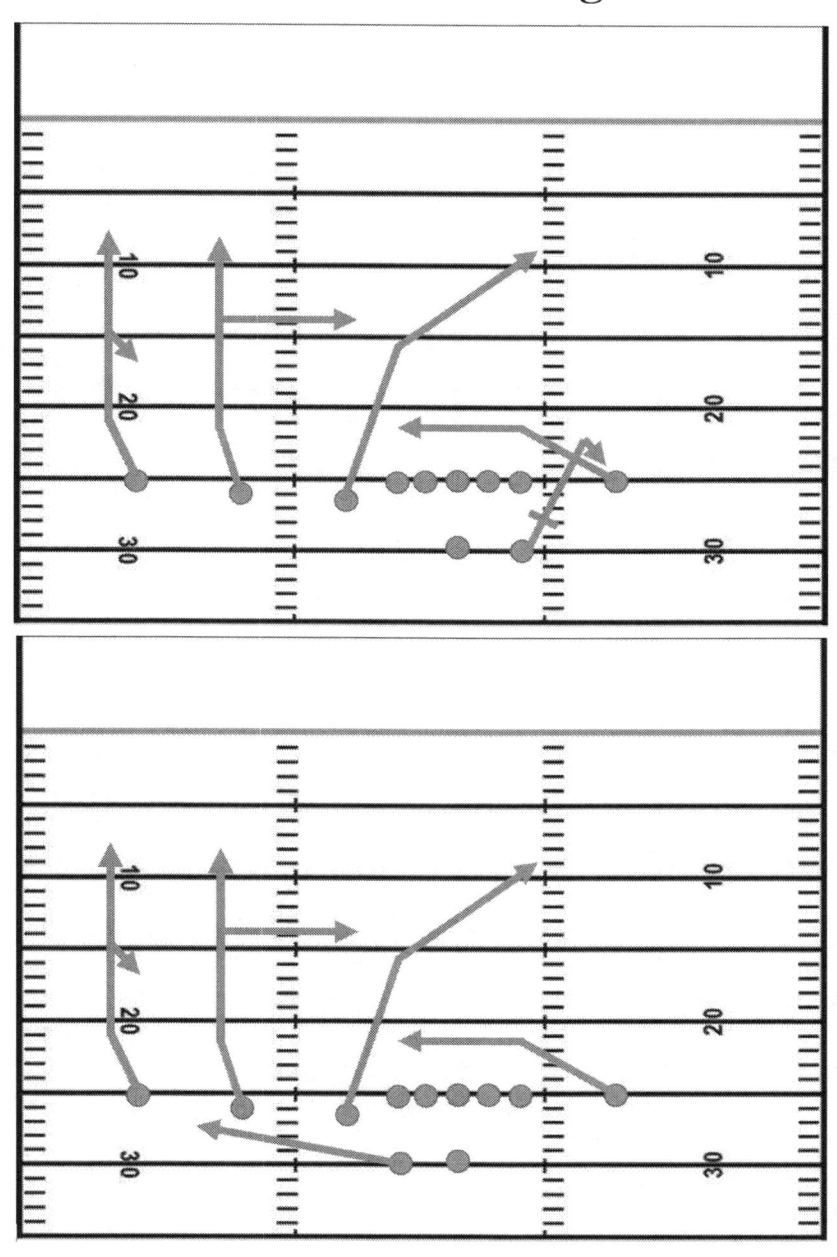

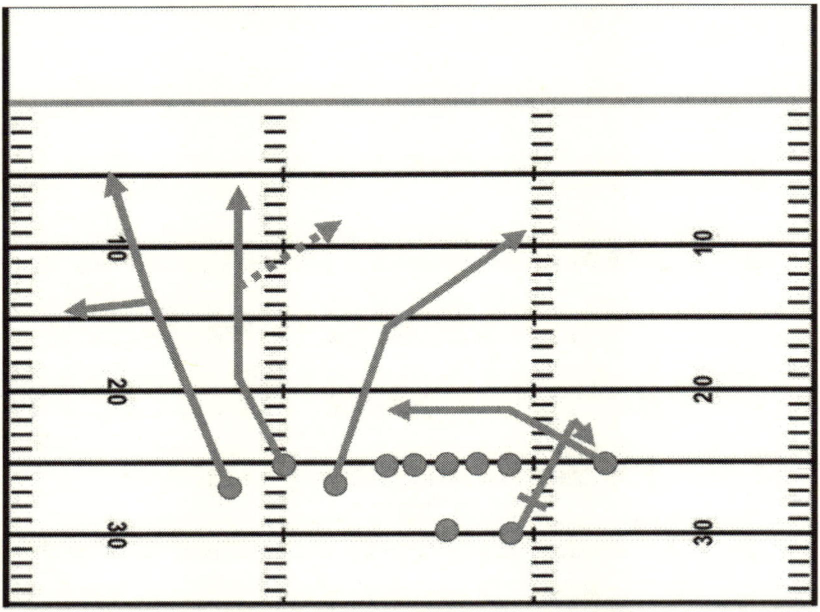
10
20
30
10
20
30

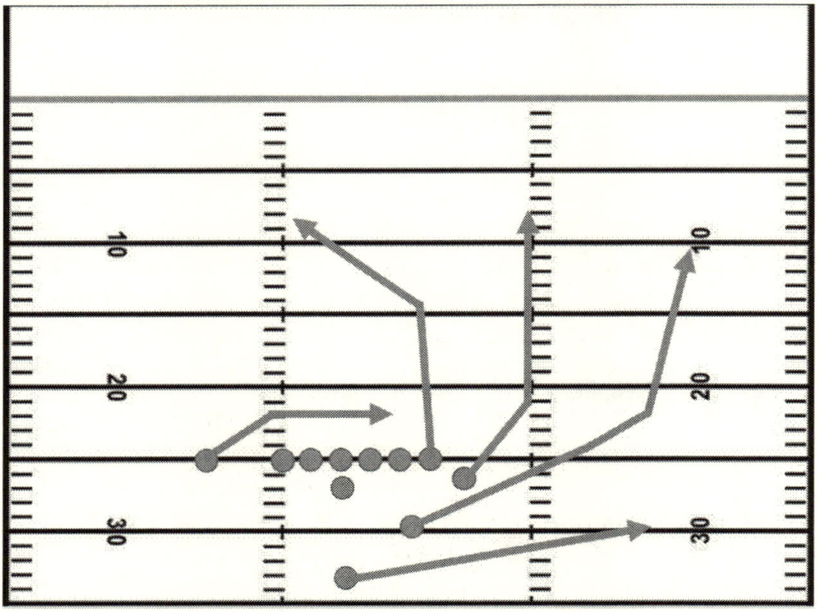
10
20
30
10
20
30

The 2018 Los Angeles Chargers Passing Index

Average Yards per Play	10.9

1st Down

Called	Average
4	13.0

Third Down (includes RZ)

Called	Success Rate
8	63%

2nd Down 6-1

Called	Average
0	0.0

2nd Down 7+

Called	Average
0	0.0

Red Zone 10-0

Called	Touchdown %
0	0%

Red Zone 10-20

Called	Touchdown %
0	0%

Week	Quarter	Time	Down	ToGo	Location	Yards
Week 1 vs KC	1	5:31	3	10	KAN 30	-6
Week 2 vs BUF	1	5:07	3	12	BUF 37	17
Week 3 vs LAR	3	14:16	3	4	LAC 31	13
Week 4 vs SF	3	1:23	3	10	LAC 40	0
Week 9 vs SEA	2	9:16	3	10	LAC 24	0
Week 11 vs DEN	1	12:27	3	6	LAC 24	27
Week 11 vs DEN	1	3:56	3	10	LAC 18	27
Week 11 vs DEN	1	3:18	1	10	LAC 45	26
Week 11 vs DEN	4	12:11	1	10	LAC 28	17
Week 11 vs DEN	4	11:26	1	10	LAC 45	6
WC vs BAL	2	0:34	1	5	RAV 41	3
WC vs BAL	3	3:36	3	9	LAC 41	12
DIV vs NE	4	12:01	3	20	LAC 14	0

Verticals - Drive

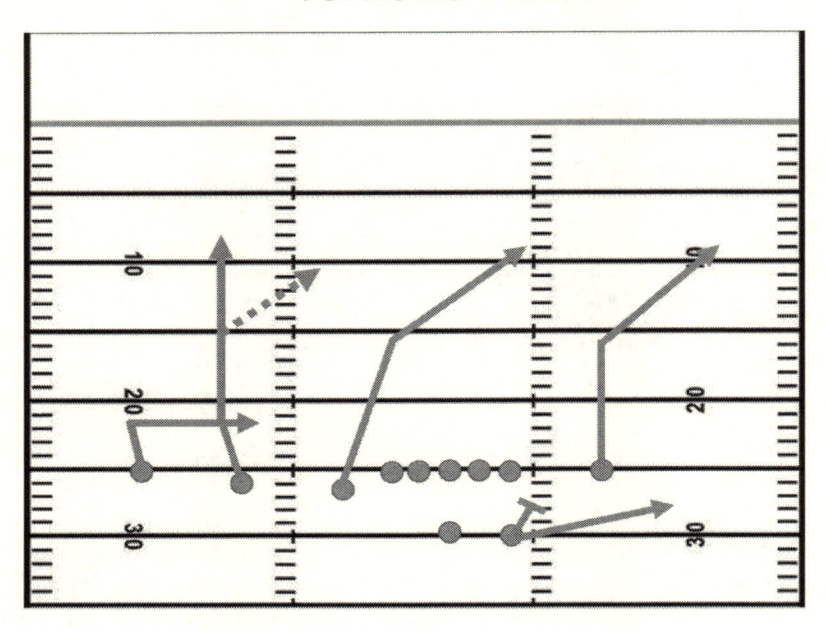

Average Yards per Play	0.8

1st Down		Third Down (includes RZ)	
Called	Average	Called	Success Rate
0	0.0	1	0%
2nd Down 6-1		2nd Down 7+	
Called	Average	Called	Average
0	0.0	0	0.0
Red Zone 10-0		Red Zone 10-20	
Called	Touchdown %	Called	Touchdown %
3	0%	0	0%

Week	Quarter	Time	Down	ToGo	Location	Yards
Week 7 vs TEN	4	12:36	3	6	OTI 10	0
Week 15 vs KC	4	0:34	2	10	KAN 10	0
Week 15 vs KC	4	4:38	2	6	KAN 9	3
DIV vs NE	4	7:51	3	4	NWE 33	0

Hank (Full Field)

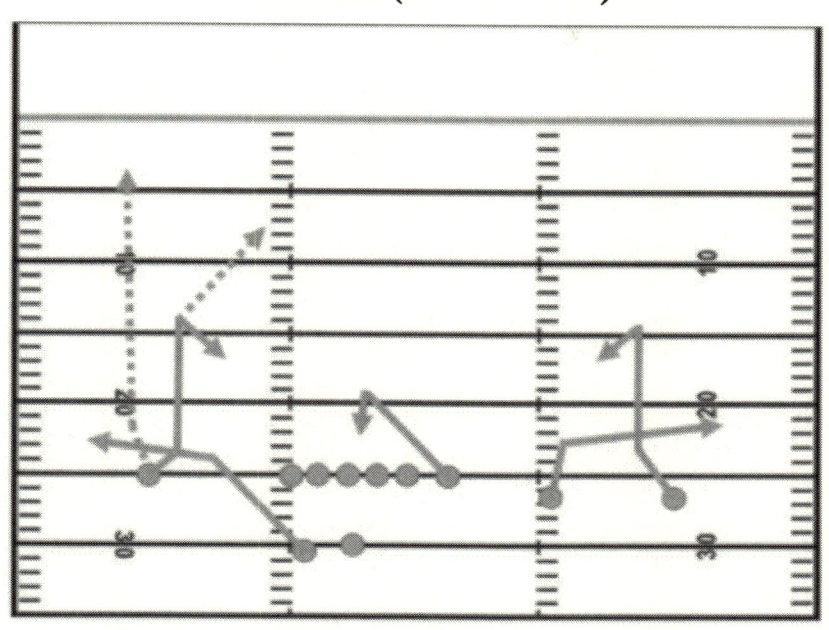

Average Yards per Play	5.4

1st Down	
Called	Average
0	0.0

Third Down (includes RZ)	
Called	Success Rate
5	20%

2nd Down 6-1	
Called	Average
0	0.0

2nd Down 7+	
Called	Average
4	5.8

Red Zone 10-0	
Called	Touchdown %
1	100%

Red Zone 10-20	
Called	Touchdown %
0	0%

Week	Quarter	Time	Down	ToGo	Location	Yards
Week 4 vs SF	1	13:15	3	7	LAC 28	0
Week 5 vs OAK	1	4:16	2	10	RAI 44	0
Week 5 vs OAK	4	11:16	3	11	RAI 31	12
Week 9 vs SEA	1	3:30	2	11	SEA 42	6
Week 9 vs SEA	3	0:04	3	8	LAC 28	0
Week 12 vs ARI	2	0:24	2	7	CRD 27	5
Week 13 vs PIT	3	1:49	2	3	PIT 10	10
Week 13 vs PIT	4	2:39	2	8	LAC 37	12
Week 16 vs BAL	2	8:29	3	15	LAC 20	0
Week 17 vs DEN	2	10:41	3	10	LAC 35	9

The 2018 Los Angeles Chargers Passing Index

All Curls

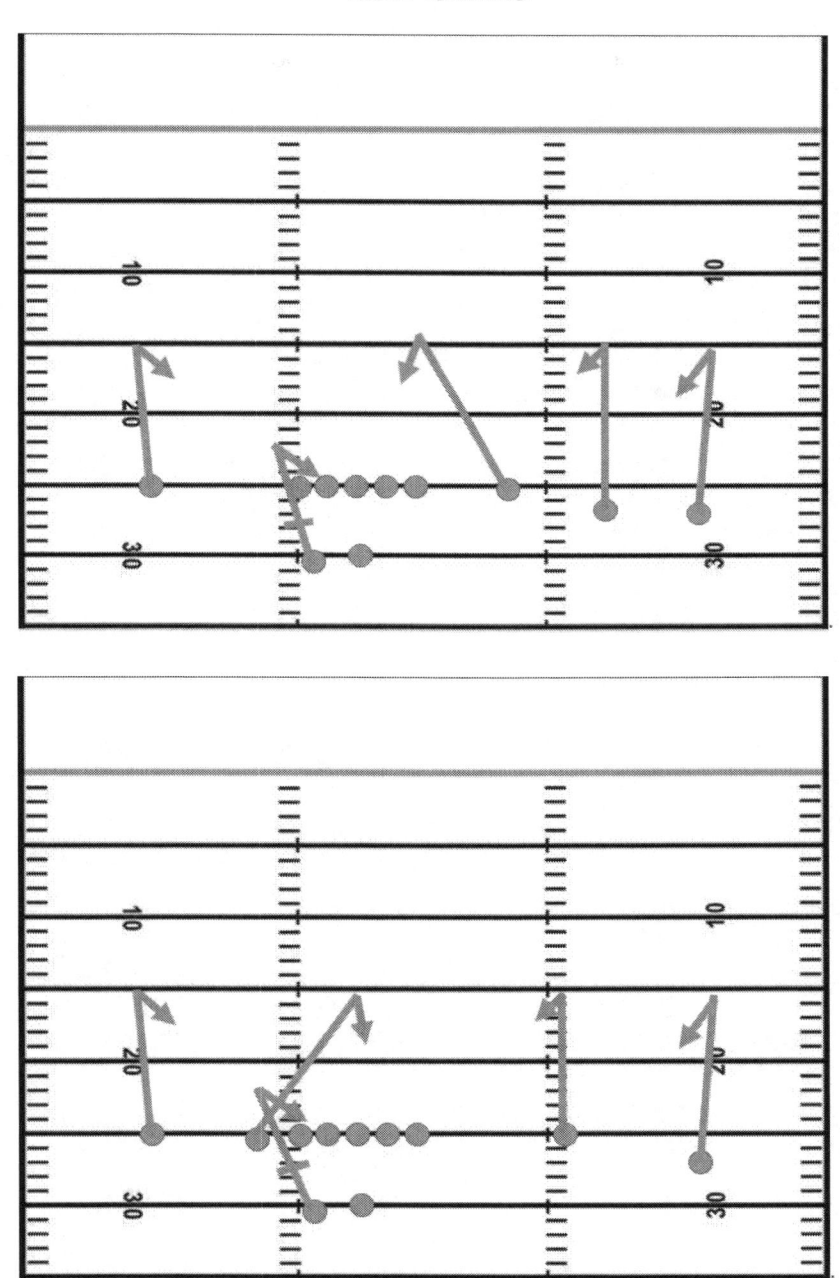

Bobby Peters

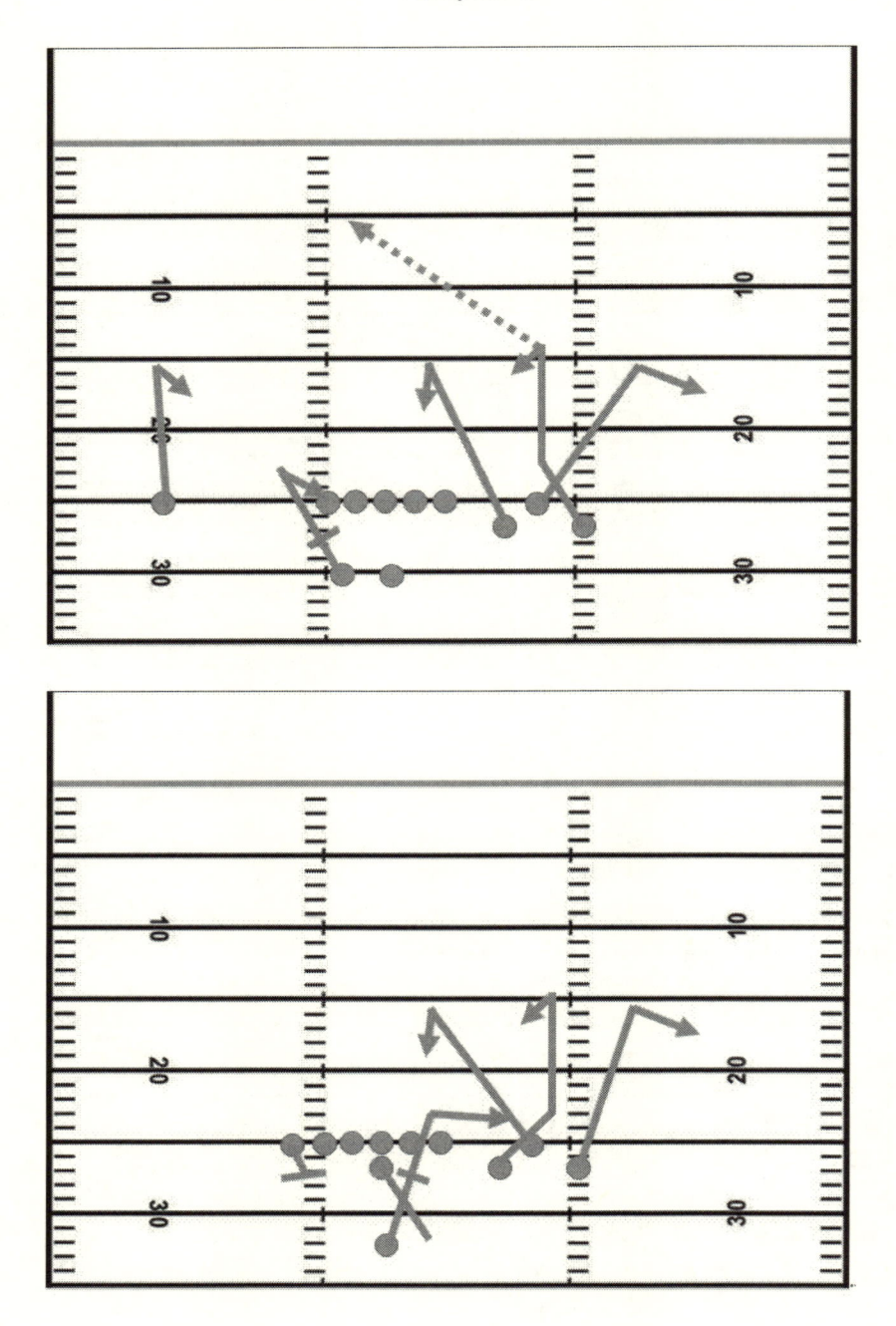

The 2018 Los Angeles Chargers Passing Index

Average Yards per Play	7.0

1st Down ||| Third Down (includes RZ)		
Called	Average	Called	Success Rate
1	0.0	3	67%

2nd Down 6-1 ||| 2nd Down 7+		
Called	Average	Called	Average
0	0.0	1	7.0

Red Zone 10-0 ||| Red Zone 10-20		
Called	Touchdown %	Called	Touchdown %
0	0%	0	0%

Week	Quarter	Time	Down	ToGo	Location	Yards
Week 7 vs TEN	4	13:46	3	4	OTI 21	7
Week 17 vs DEN	3	9:01	3	13	LAC 19	16
WC vs BAL	2	11:20	2	9	LAC 32	7
DIV vs NE	1	0:42	3	9	LAC 26	0
DIV vs NE	3	5:15	1	10	NWE 37	5

Dotted "Post" tag used in 1Q DIV vs NE

Bobby Peters

Drive Variations

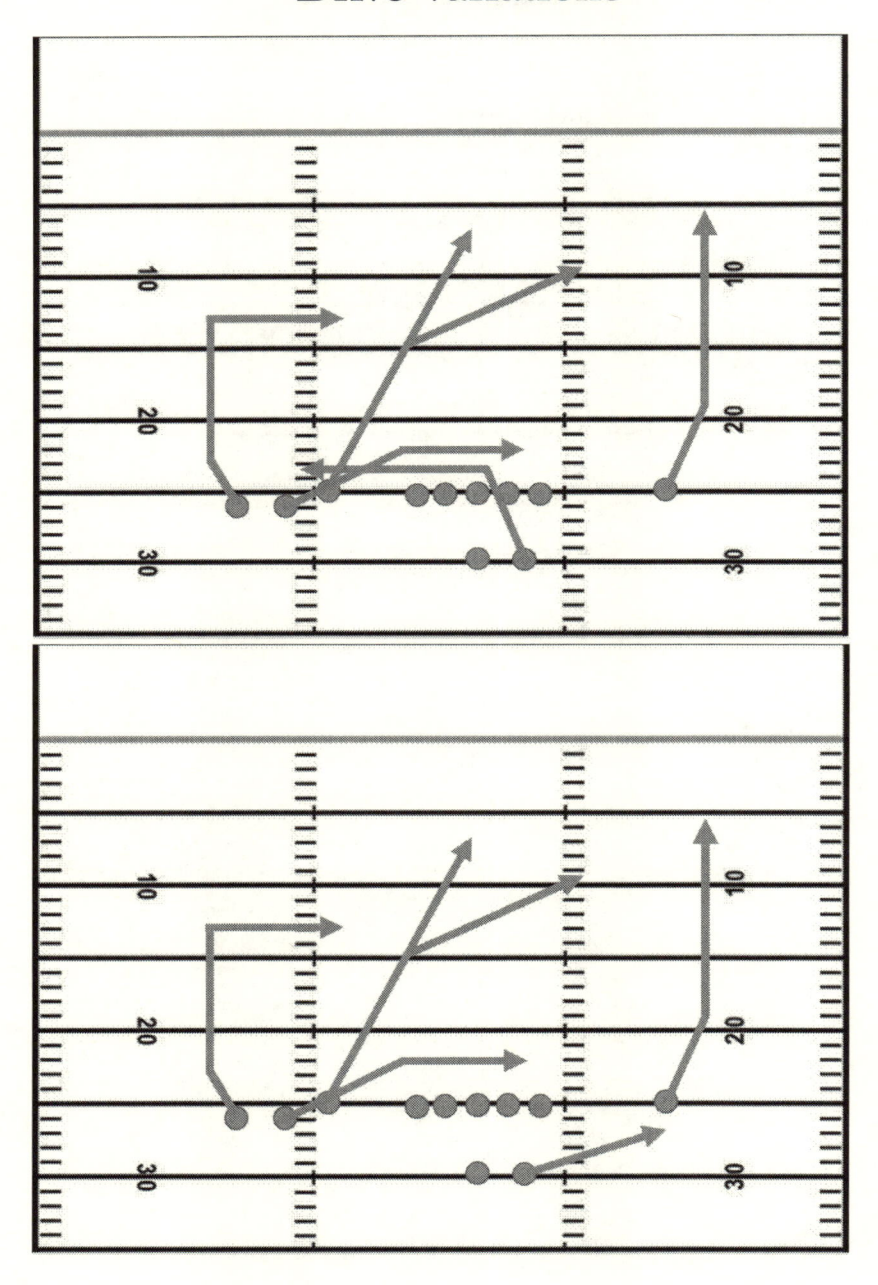

The 2018 Los Angeles Chargers Passing Index

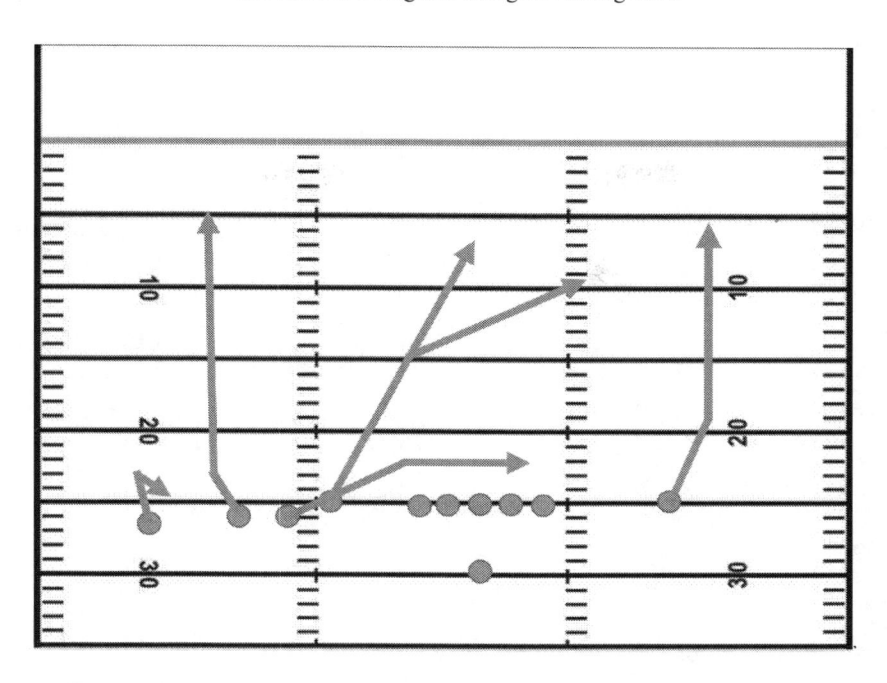

Average Yards per Play	6.7

1st Down	
Called	Average
3	9.3

Third Down (includes RZ)	
Called	Success Rate
9	33%

2nd Down 6-1	
Called	Average
0	0.0

2nd Down 7+	
Called	Average
4	6.0

Red Zone 10-0	
Called	Touchdown %
0	0%

Red Zone 10-20	
Called	Touchdown %
0	0%

Week	Quarter	Time	Down	ToGo	Location	Yards
Week 1 vs KC	1	10:03	3	8	KAN 31	4
Week 1 vs KC	1	1:14	3	11	KAN 30	9
Week 4 vs SF	3	1:30	2	10	LAC 40	0
Week 10 vs OAK	1	6:42	3	5	LAC 6	0
Week 10 vs OAK	3	7:35	3	4	LAC 31	TO
Week 11 vs DEN	1	13:12	2	9	LAC 21	3
Week 13 vs PIT	4	11:53	2	10	LAC 21	14
Week 14 vs CIN	2	4:09	3	10	LAC 17	0
Week 14 vs CIN	2	0:10	1	10	LAC 32	11
Week 14 vs CIN	4	8:29	2	10	CIN 21	7
Week 16 vs BAL	4	9:01	3	14	LAC 38	17
Week 16 vs BAL	4	7:35	3	6	RAV 41	7
Week 17 vs DEN	1	6:42	1	10	LAC 11	17
DIV vs NE	1	6:52	3	15	LAC 28	18
DIV vs NE	2	4:33	3	10	LAC 47	0
DIV vs NE	3	14:53	1	10	LAC 31	0

Shallow Cross

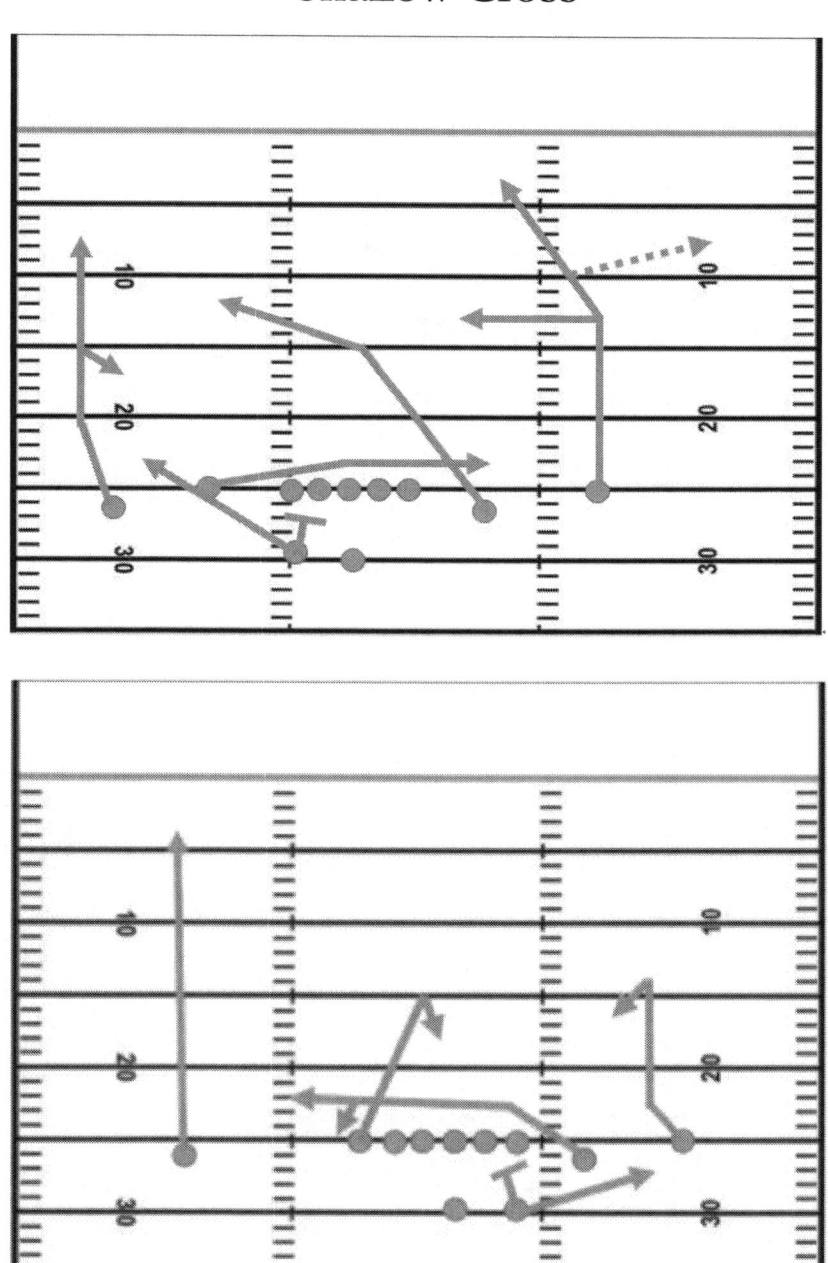

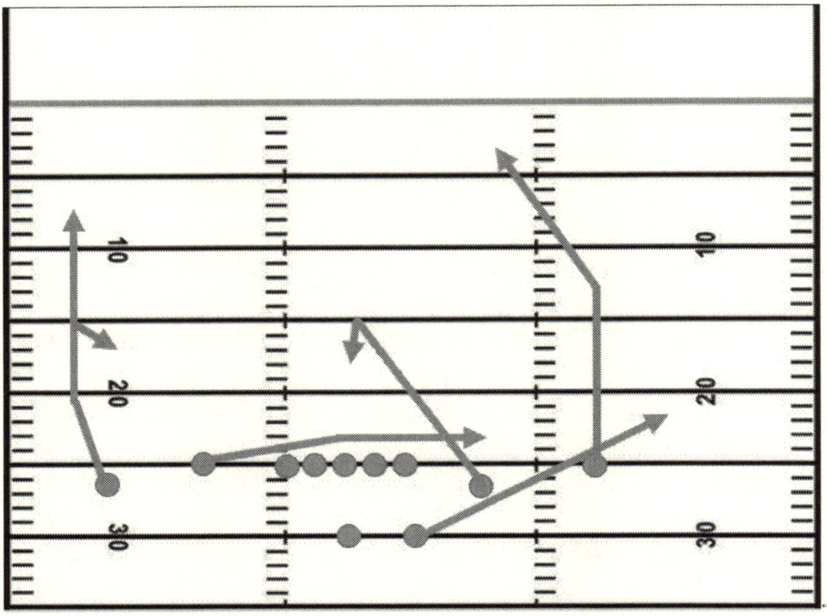

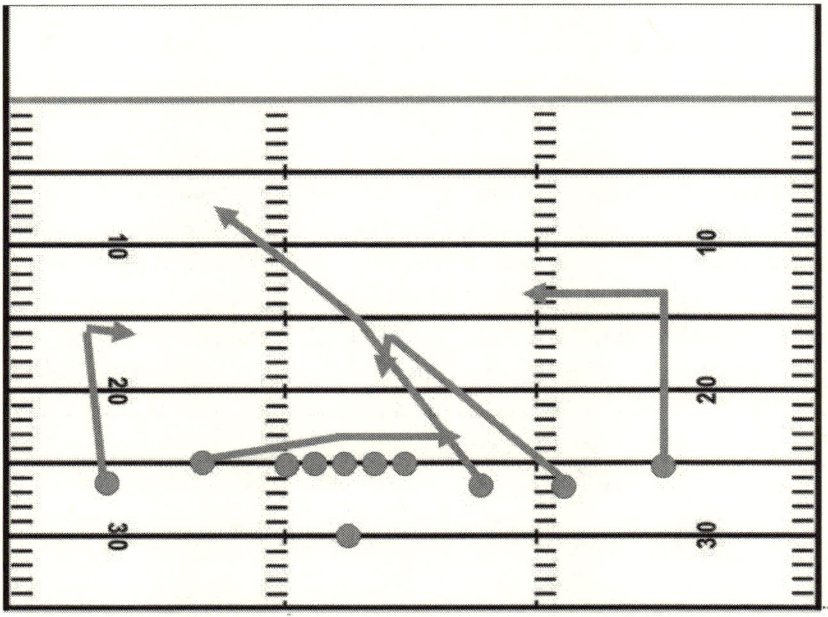

The 2018 Los Angeles Chargers Passing Index

Average Yards per Play	5.2

1st Down

Called	Average
2	12.0

Third Down (includes RZ)

Called	Success Rate
5	40%

2nd Down 6-1

Called	Average
3	-2.7

2nd Down 7+

Called	Average
4	6.3

Red Zone 10-0

Called	Touchdown %
0	0%

Red Zone 10-20

Called	Touchdown %
0	0%

Week	Quarter	Time	Down	ToGo	Location	Yards
Week 2 vs BUF	2	7:15	2	7	LAC 33	8
Week 2 vs BUF	4	8:17	3	9	BUF 39	6
Week 3 vs LAR	1	12:26	2	5	LAC 29	0
Week 3 vs LAR	1	0:08	2	9	LAC 26	3
Week 4 vs SF	1	10:24	3	5	LAC 42	4
Week 7 vs TEN	3	14:29	1	10	LAC 38	7
Week 10 vs OAK	4	7:52	3	11	RAI 22	0
Week 11 vs DEN	3	3:59	2	9	DEN 35	0
Week 13 vs PIT	3	3:13	3	14	PIT 35	18
Week 14 vs CIN	2	1:56	2	1	LAC 16	0
Week 16 vs BAL	4	9:45	2	6	LAC 46	-8
Week 16 vs BAL	4	2:00	1	10	LAC 40	17
WC vs BAL	2	0:40	2	10	LAC 40	14
WC vs BAL	4	11:45	3	8	RAV 43	9
DIV vs NE	4	12:13	1	20	LAC 14	0

Bobby Peters

Middle Read

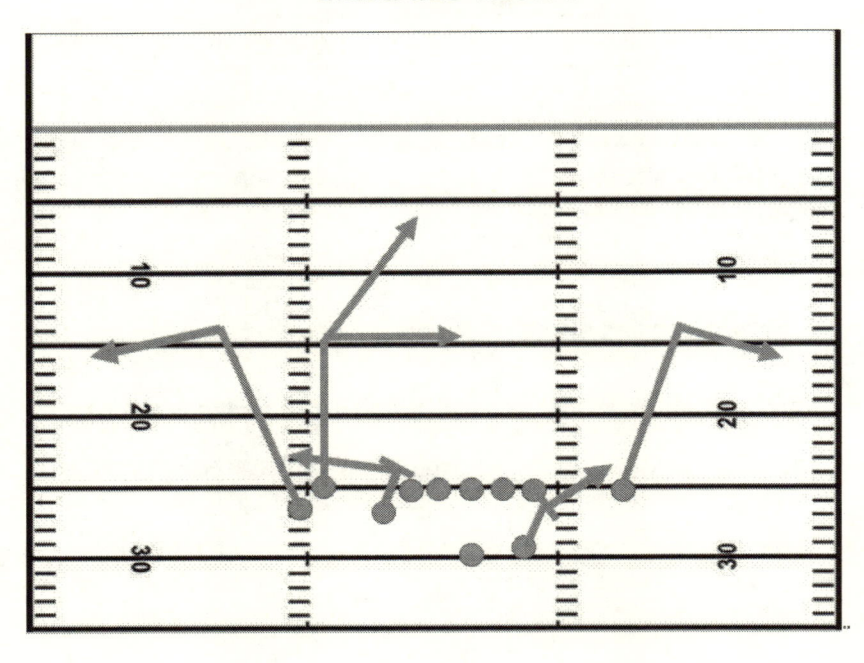

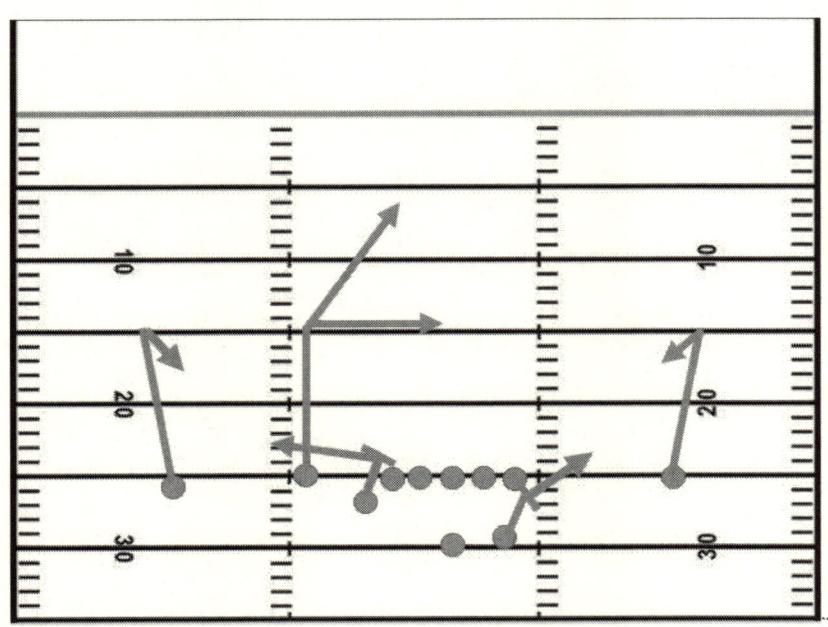

The 2018 Los Angeles Chargers Passing Index

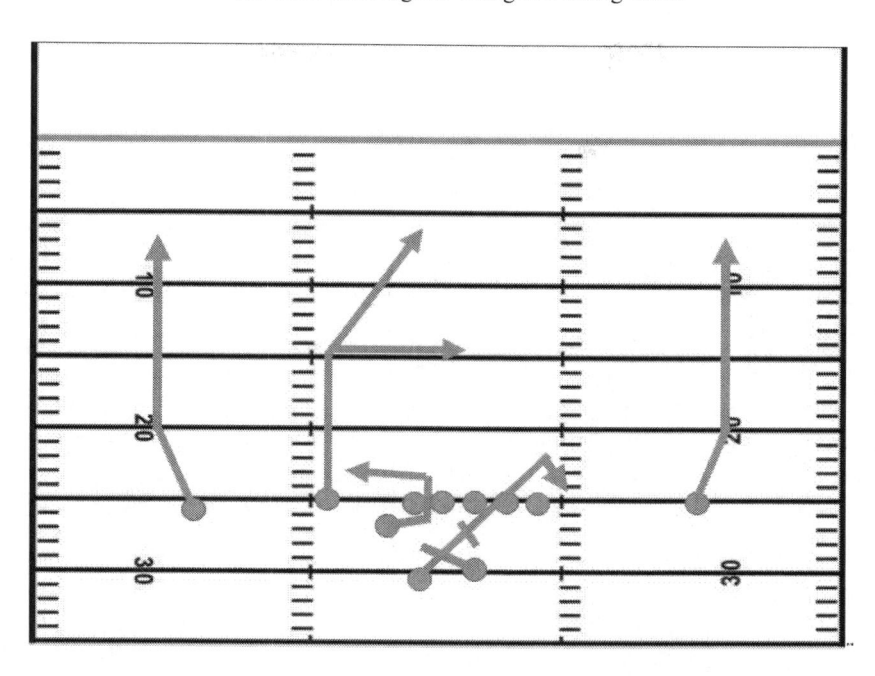

Average Yards per Play	11.6

1st Down		Third Down (includes RZ)	
Called	Average	Called	Success Rate
3	4.7	6	67%
2nd Down 6-1		2nd Down 7+	
Called	Average	Called	Average
0	0.0	2	5.0
Red Zone 10-0		Red Zone 10-20	
Called	Touchdown %	Called	Touchdown %
0	0%	0	0%

Week	Quarter	Time	Down	ToGo	Location	Yards
Week 3 vs LAR	2	5:28	3	17	RAM 49	25
Week 4 vs SF	3	3:50	3	13	LAC 37	0
Week 4 vs SF	4	10:38	1	10	SFO 45	7
Week 9 vs SEA	2	12:29	3	15	LAC 12	54
Week 10 vs OAK	4	14:42	1	10	LAC 21	7
Week 11 vs DEN	1	8:25	1	20	DEN 30	0
Week 13 vs PIT	4	4:06	2	10	LAC 25	10
Week 15 vs KC	2	1:07	3	12	KAN 24	13
Week 17 vs DEN	1	13:25	3	6	DEN 39	TO
Week 17 vs DEN	1	8:35	2	8	DEN 49	0
WC vs BAL	3	13:57	3	7	RAV 23	0

The 2018 Los Angeles Chargers Passing Index

Y Cross

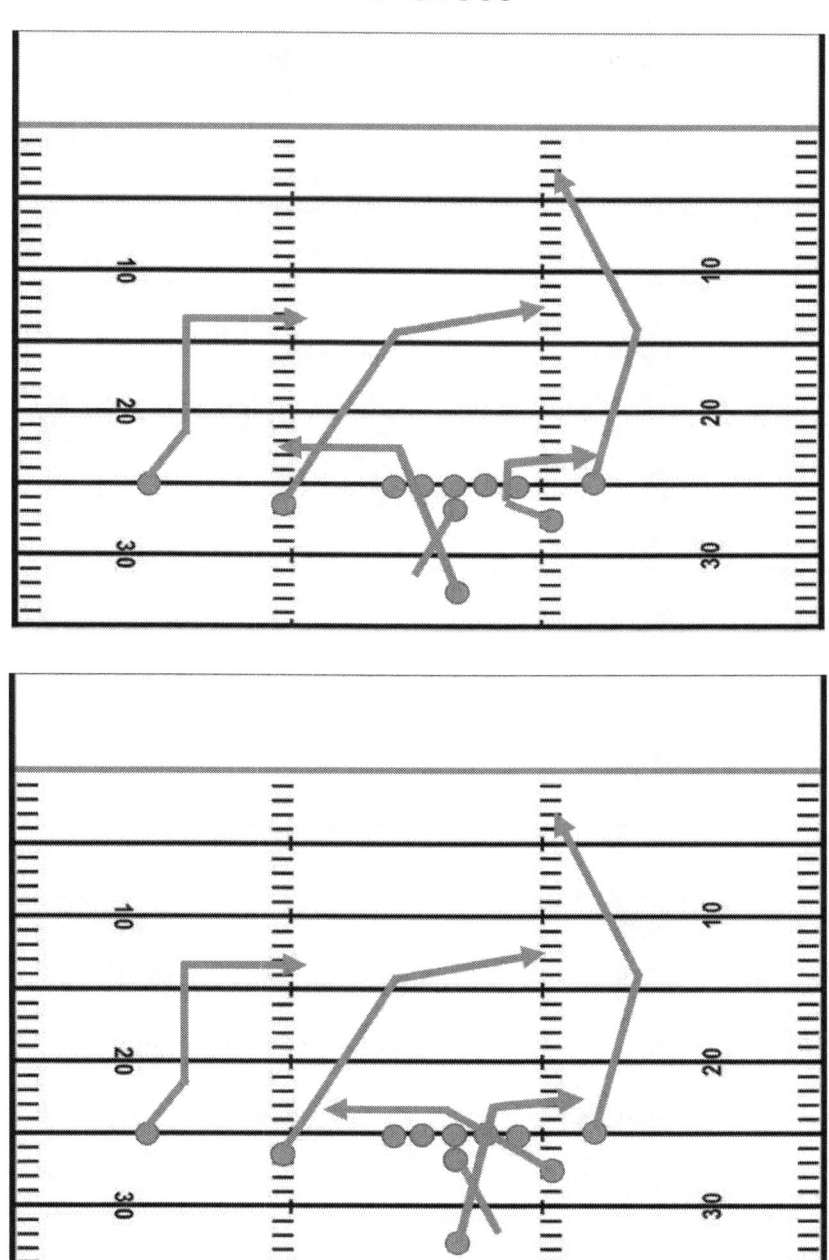

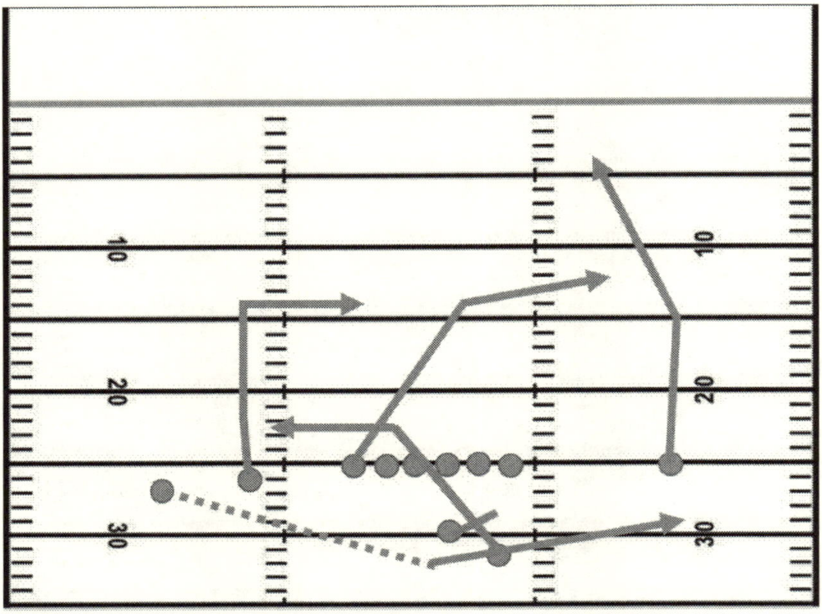
10
20
30
10
20
30

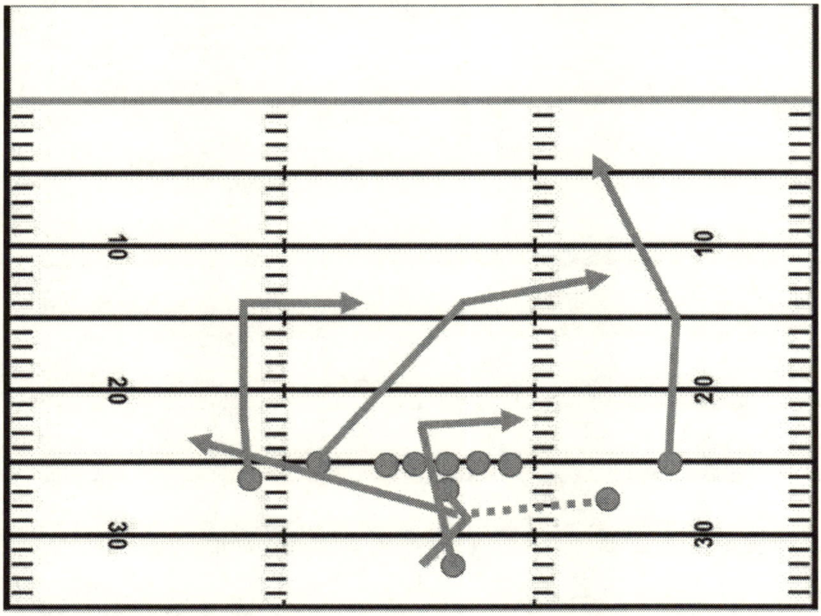
10
20
30
10
20
30

The 2018 Los Angeles Chargers Passing Index

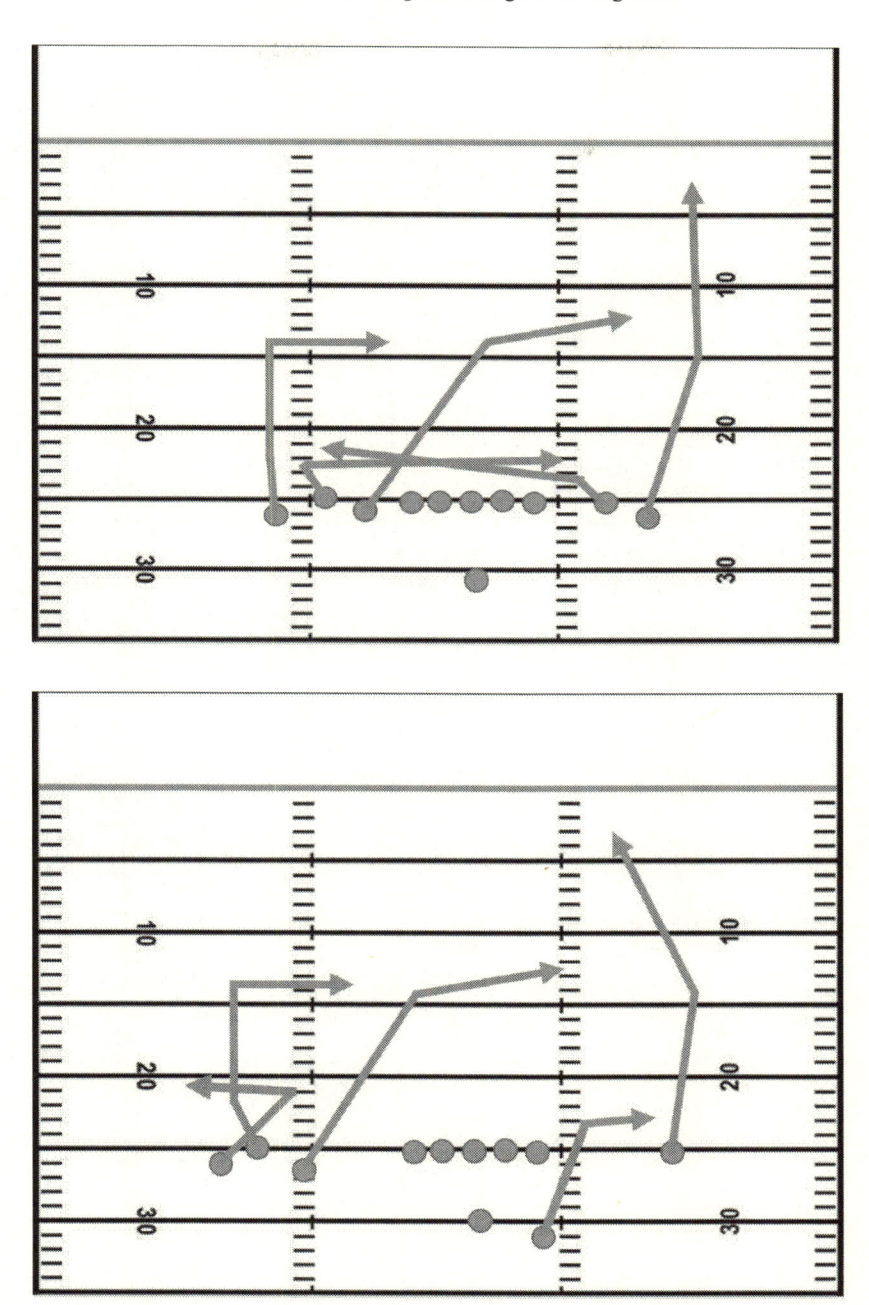

Average Yards per Play	3.8

1st Down	
Called	Average
7	5.3

Third Down (includes RZ)	
Called	Success Rate
3	67%

2nd Down 6-1	
Called	Average
1	1.0

2nd Down 7+	
Called	Average
2	-1.0

Red Zone 10-0	
Called	Touchdown %
0	0%

Red Zone 10-20	
Called	Touchdown %
0	0%

Week	Quarter	Time	Down	ToGo	Location	Yards
Week 3 vs LAR	4	14:17	3	4	RAM 29	5
Week 5 vs OAK	3	9:56	2	11	RAI 37	0
Week 6 vs CLE	3	12:47	3	10	LAC 44	-12
Week 9 vs SEA	2	1:23	1	10	SEA 30	0
Week 9 vs SEA	3	14:54	1	10	LAC 16	16
Week 10 vs OAK	2	10:37	2	6	RAI 36	1
Week 12 vs ARI	3	6:04	1	10	LAC 27	0
Week 12 vs ARI	3	3:48	1	10	CRD 39	15
Week 13 vs PIT	1	12:42	2	9	PIT 42	-2
Week 15 vs KC	2	6:29	1	10	LAC 35	-5
Week 16 vs BAL	4	2:54	1	20	RAV 49	11
Week 17 vs DEN	1	14:14	1	10	DEN 43	0
Week 17 vs DEN	4	6:23	3	5	DEN 22	21

The 2018 Los Angeles Chargers Passing Index

U / X / Z Cross

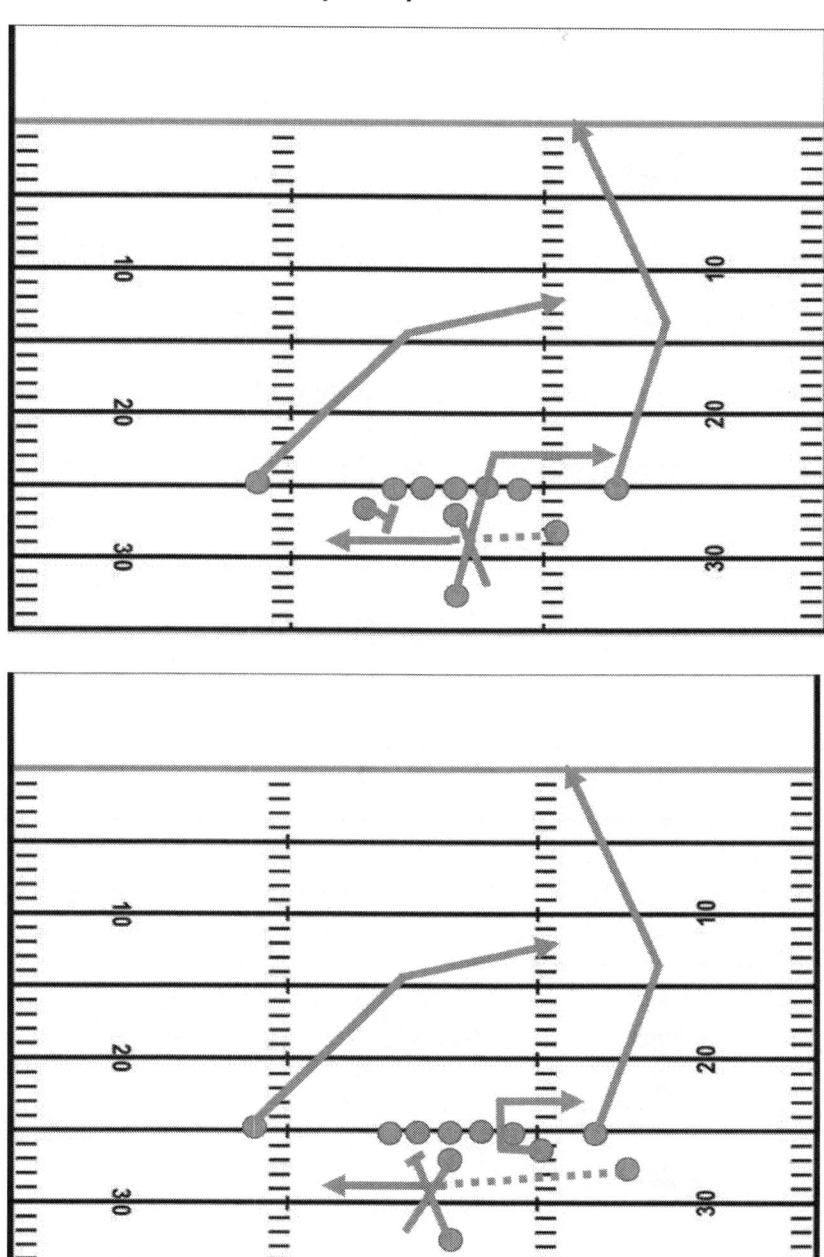

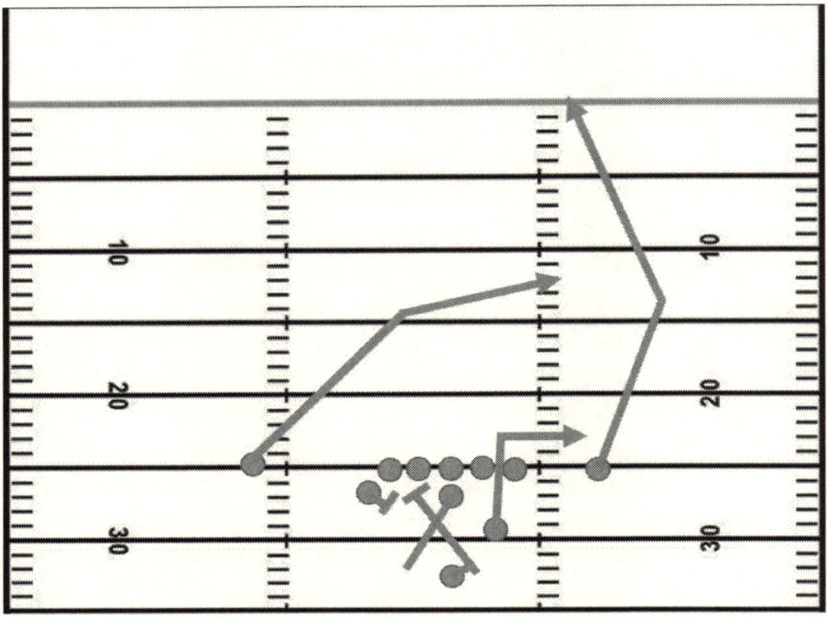
10
20
30
10
20
30

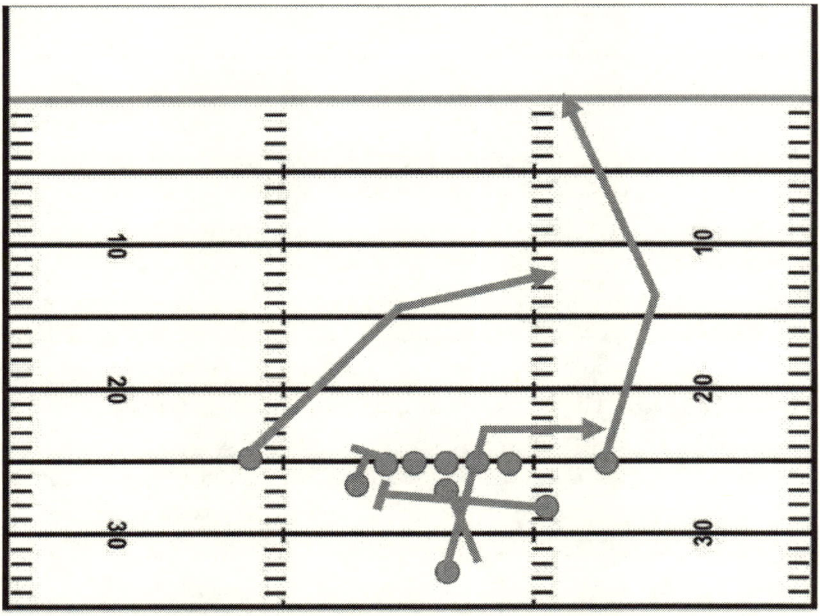
10
20
30
10
20
30

The 2018 Los Angeles Chargers Passing Index

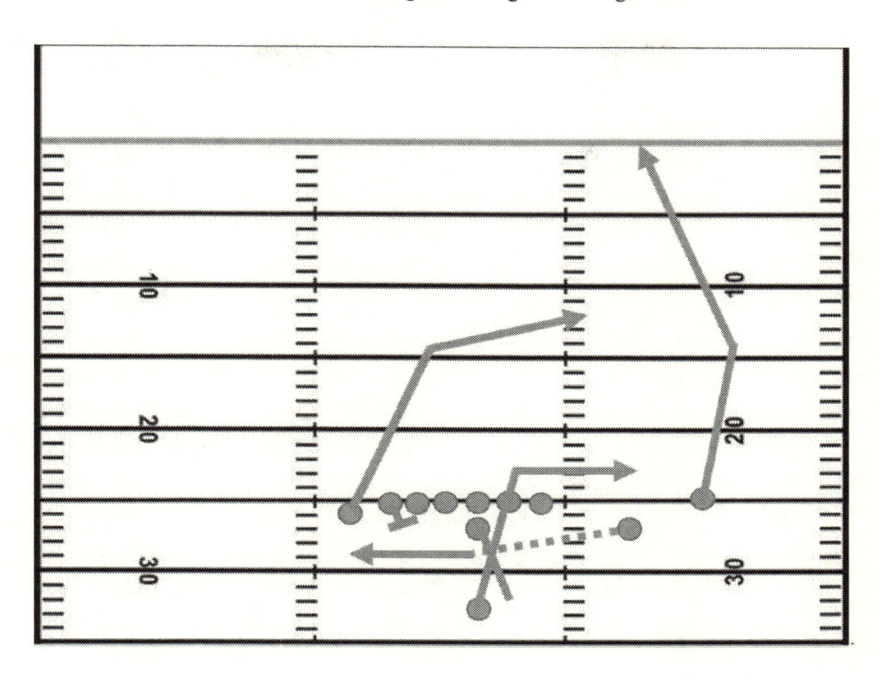

Average Yards per Play	11.9

1st Down		Third Down (includes RZ)	
Called	Average	Called	Success Rate
20	11.4	0	0%
2nd Down 6-1		2nd Down 7+	
Called	Average	Called	Average
1	3.0	4	16.5
Red Zone 10-0		Red Zone 10-20	
Called	Touchdown %	Called	Touchdown %
0	0%	0	0%

Week	Quarter	Time	Down	ToGo	Location	Yards
Week 1 vs KC	2	11:07	1	10	LAC 41	25
Week 1 vs KC	2	10:21	1	10	KAN 34	0
Week 2 vs BUF	4	11:23	2	14	LAC 34	16
Week 3 vs LAR	1	4:50	2	12	RAM 42	42
Week 3 vs LAR	1	0:51	1	10	LAC 25	1
Week 3 vs LAR	4	6:59	1	10	RAM 37	15
Week 4 vs SF	1	9:08	1	10	LAC 47	13
Week 4 vs SF	1	3:53	1	10	LAC 25	18
Week 4 vs SF	1	2:36	1	10	SFO 35	5
Week 4 vs SF	3	5:54	1	10	LAC 25	15
Week 4 vs SF	3	1:35	1	10	LAC 40	0
Week 5 vs OAK	1	7:49	1	10	LAC 21	10
Week 5 vs OAK	3	8:35	1	20	RAI 31	9
Week 7 vs TEN	1	4:52	1	10	LAC 43	24
Week 7 vs TEN	3	8:13	1	10	LAC 37	6
Week 7 vs TEN	4	8:21	1	10	LAC 41	-1
Week 10 vs OAK	2	3:33	1	10	LAC 9	5
Week 10 vs OAK	2	2:29	1	10	LAC 45	18
Week 10 vs OAK	4	10:44	1	20	RAI 43	18
Week 11 vs DEN	1	9:42	1	10	DEN 34	0
Week 14 vs CIN	1	4:26	1	10	LAC 36	10
Week 14 vs CIN	4	12:06	1	10	LAC 25	37
Week 15 vs KC	2	4:18	2	7	KAN 41	8
Week 15 vs KC	3	7:29	2	4	KAN 40	3
DIV vs NE	1	6:59	2	10	LAC 33	0

X / Z Cross - Drag

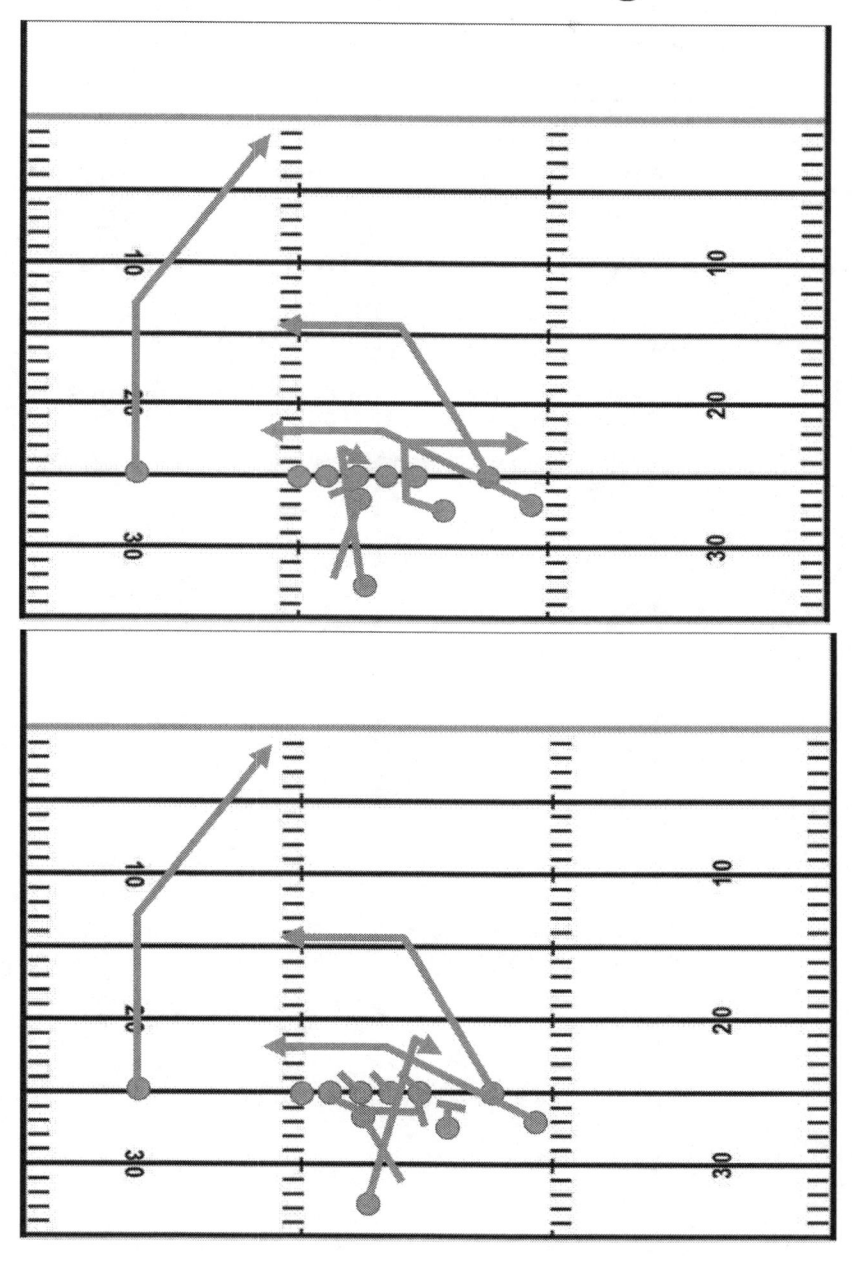

Average Yards per Play	3.2

1st Down		Third Down (includes RZ)	
Called	Average	Called	Success Rate
3	0.3	0	0%
2nd Down 6-1		2nd Down 7+	
Called	Average	Called	Average
1	22.0	1	-7.0
Red Zone 10-0		Red Zone 10-20	
Called	Touchdown %	Called	Touchdown %
0	0%	0	0%

Week	Quarter	Time	Down	ToGo	Location	Yards
Week 2 vs BUF	3	2:04	2	10	LAC 25	-7
Week 4 vs SF	1	1:55	2	5	SFO 30	22
Week 7 vs TEN	3	8:13	1	10	LAC 37	6
Week 11 vs DEN	2	10:27	1	10	LAC 42	-5
Week 15 vs KC	2	7:20	1	10	LAC 19	0

Play Action - Dagger

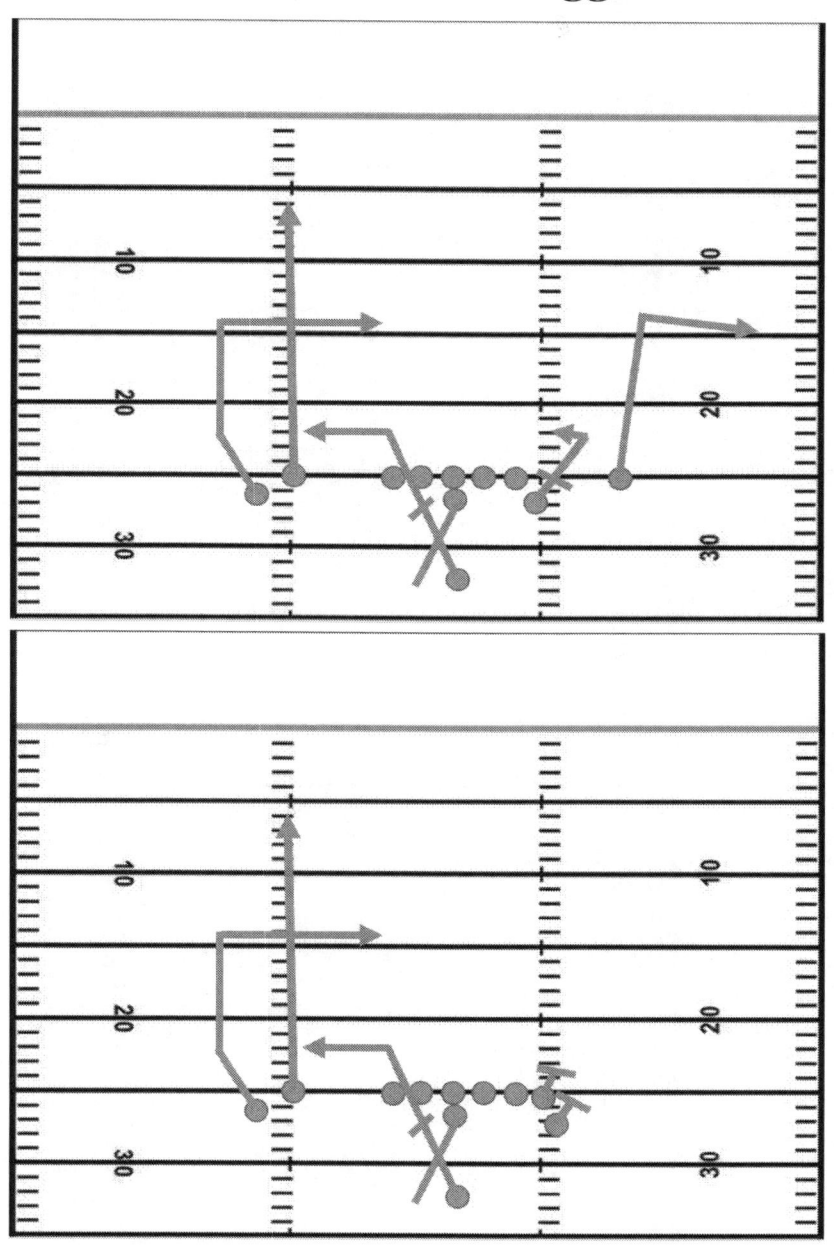

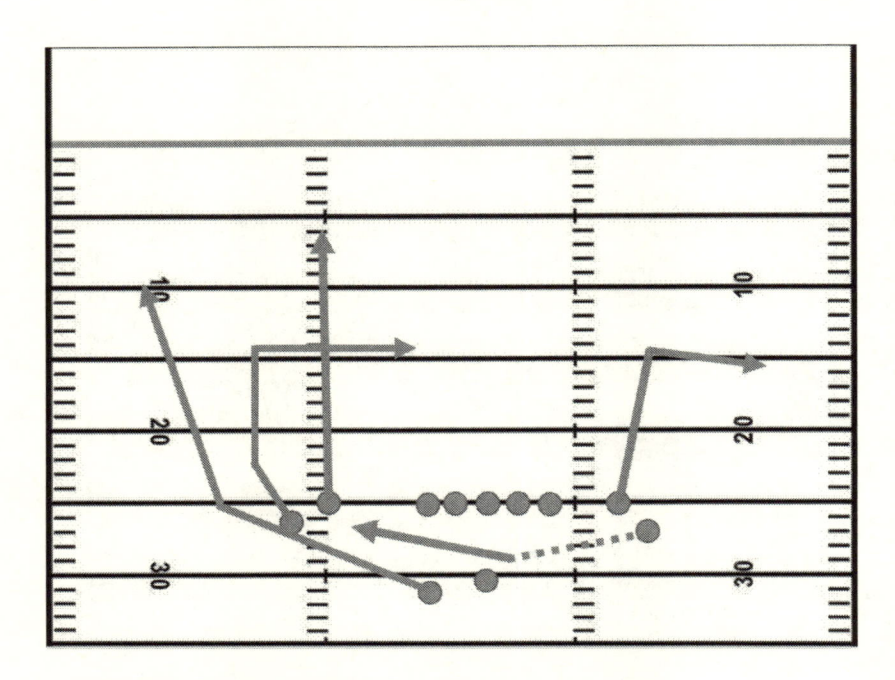

Average Yards per Play — 11.3

1st Down		Third Down (includes RZ)	
Called	Average	Called	Success Rate
2	19.5	0	0%
2nd Down 6-1		**2nd Down 7+**	
Called	Average	Called	Average
2	8.5	2	11.5
Red Zone 10-0		**Red Zone 10-20**	
Called	Touchdown %	Called	Touchdown %
0	0%	1	0%

The 2018 Los Angeles Chargers Passing Index

Week	Quarter	Time	Down	ToGo	Location	Yards
Week 5 vs OAK	1	14:18	2	5	LAC 37	17
Week 5 vs OAK	4	13:49	2	18	LAC 44	26
Week 9 vs SEA	4	8:50	2	12	LAC 40	-3
Week 10 vs OAK	2	8:38	2	6	RAI 19	0
Week 13 vs PIT	3	6:29	1	10	PIT 47	-4
Week 16 vs BAL	4	7:39	2	6	RAV 41	0
DIV vs NE	**1**	**5:03**	**1**	**10**	**NWE 43**	**43**

Double move bolded (DIV vs NE)

Bunch Dagger

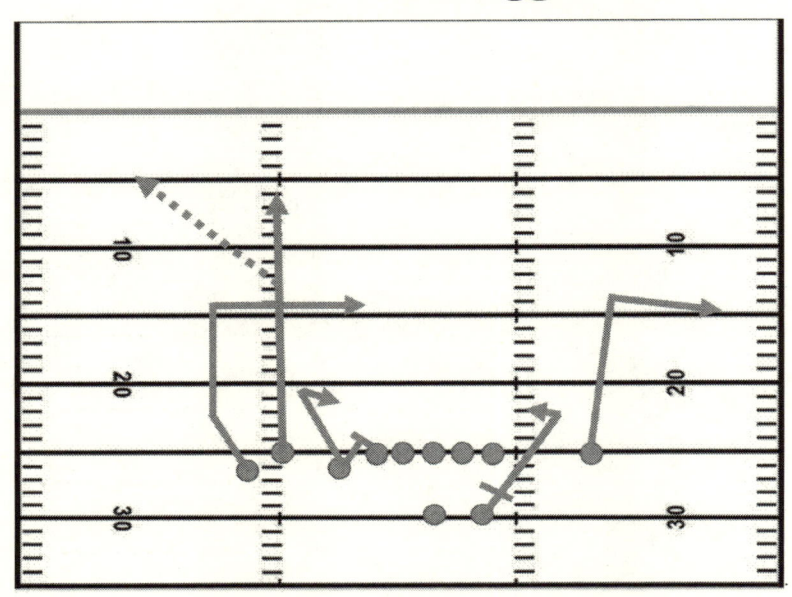

Average Yards per Play	2.7

1st Down		Third Down (includes RZ)	
Called	Average	Called	Success Rate
0	0.0	2	50%
2nd Down 6-1		2nd Down 7+	
Called	Average	Called	Average
0	0.0	0	0.0
Red Zone 10-0		Red Zone 10-20	
Called	Touchdown %	Called	Touchdown %
0	0%	1	0%

Week	Quarter	Time	Down	ToGo	Location	Yards
Week 2 vs BUF	3	4:41	3	7	LAC 15	-9
Week 10 vs OAK	2	8:38	2	6	RAI 19	0
Week 14 vs CIN	4	9:54	3	10	CIN 38	17

The 2018 Los Angeles Chargers Passing Index

Bunch Dagger - Whip

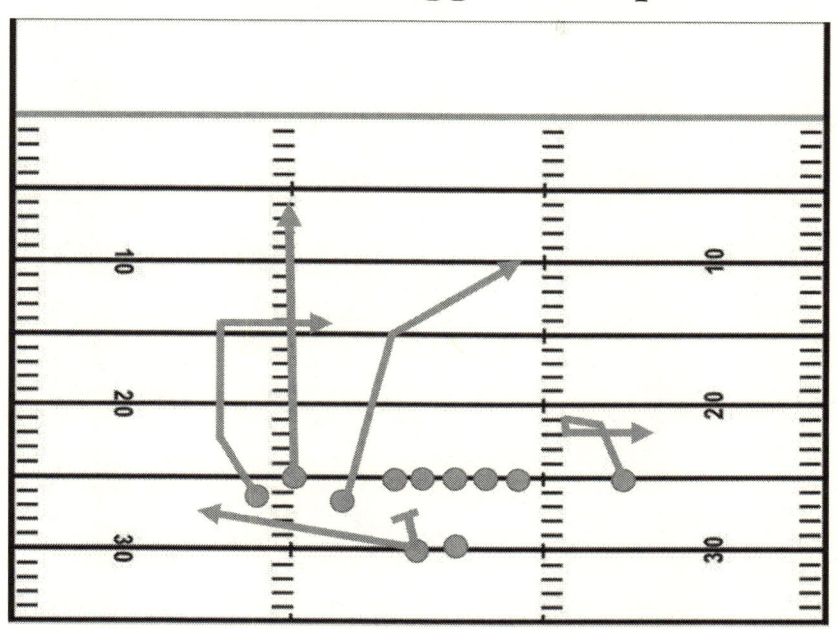

Average Yards per Play	5.5

1st Down		Third Down (includes RZ)	
Called	Average	Called	Success Rate
0	0.0	4	50%
2nd Down 6-1		2nd Down 7+	
Called	Average	Called	Average
0	0.0	0	0.0
Red Zone 10-0		Red Zone 10-20	
Called	Touchdown %	Called	Touchdown %
0	0%	0	0%

Week	Quarter	Time	Down	ToGo	Location	Yards
Week 7 vs TEN	2	9:57	3	4	OTI 48	0
Week 10 vs OAK	2	9:58	3	5	RAI 35	12
Week 11 vs DEN	1	10:22	3	2	DEN 41	7
DIV vs NE	3	14:44	3	10	LAC 31	3

Bunch Dagger - Drag

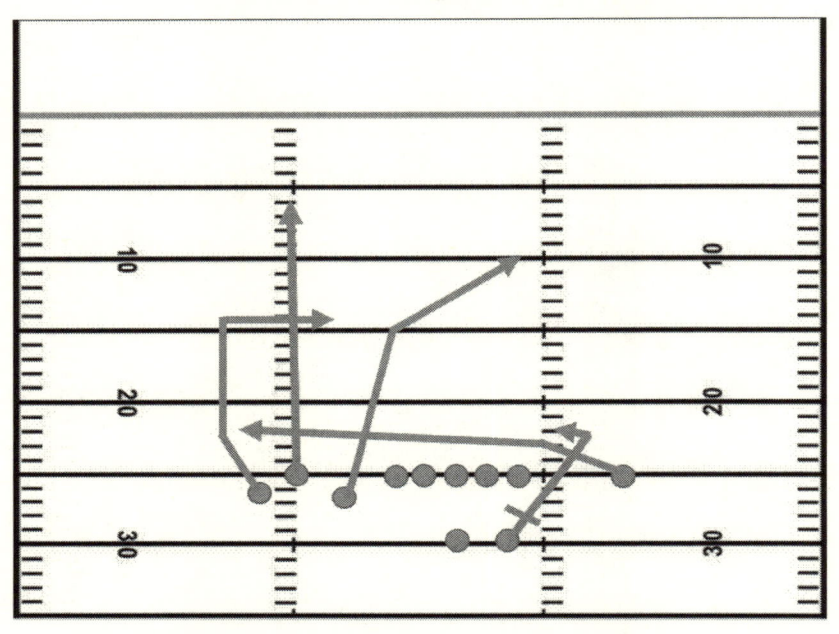

Average Yards per Play	18.0

1st Down		Third Down (includes RZ)	
Called	Average	Called	Success Rate
0	0.0	1	100%
2nd Down 6-1		2nd Down 7+	
Called	Average	Called	Average
0	0.0	1	23.0
Red Zone 10-0		Red Zone 10-20	
Called	Touchdown %	Called	Touchdown %
0	0%	0	0%

Week	Quarter	Time	Down	ToGo	Location	Yards
Week 1 vs KC	4	8:36	2	19	LAC 16	23
Week 7 vs TEN	3	0:39	3	7	OTI 40	13

The 2018 Los Angeles Chargers Passing Index

Post – Comeback Double Move

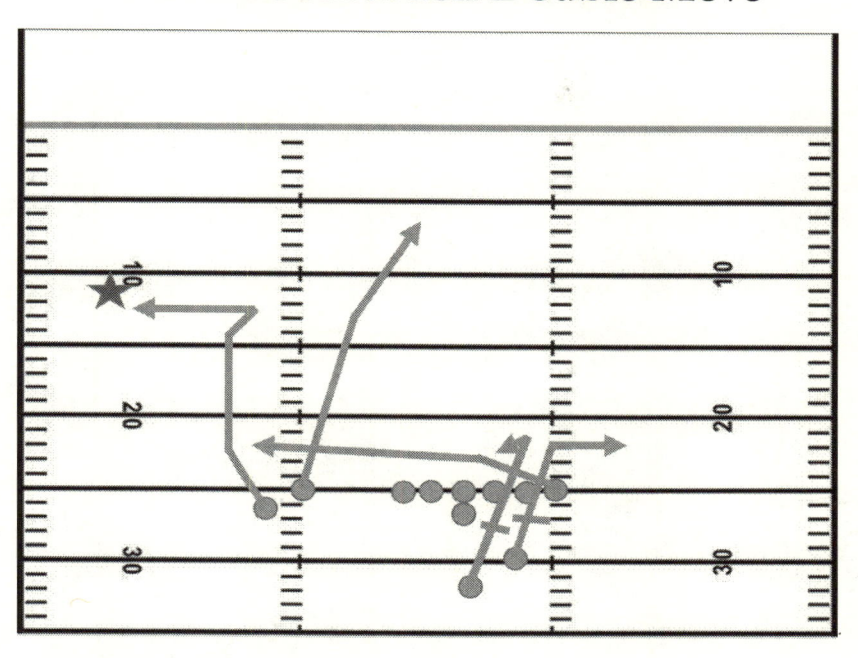

Average Yards per Play	2.7

1st Down		Third Down (includes RZ)	
Called	Average	Called	Success Rate
0	0.0	1	0%
2nd Down 6-1		**2nd Down 7+**	
Called	Average	Called	Average
1	17.0	1	-9.0
Red Zone 10-0		**Red Zone 10-20**	
Called	Touchdown %	Called	Touchdown %
0	0%	0	0%

Week	Quarter	Time	Down	ToGo	Location	Yards
Week 5 vs OAK	1	14:18	2	5	LAC 37	17
Week 10 vs OAK	4	7:52	3	11	RAI 22	0
Week 13 vs PIT	1	8:39	2	10	LAC 21	-9

Mesh

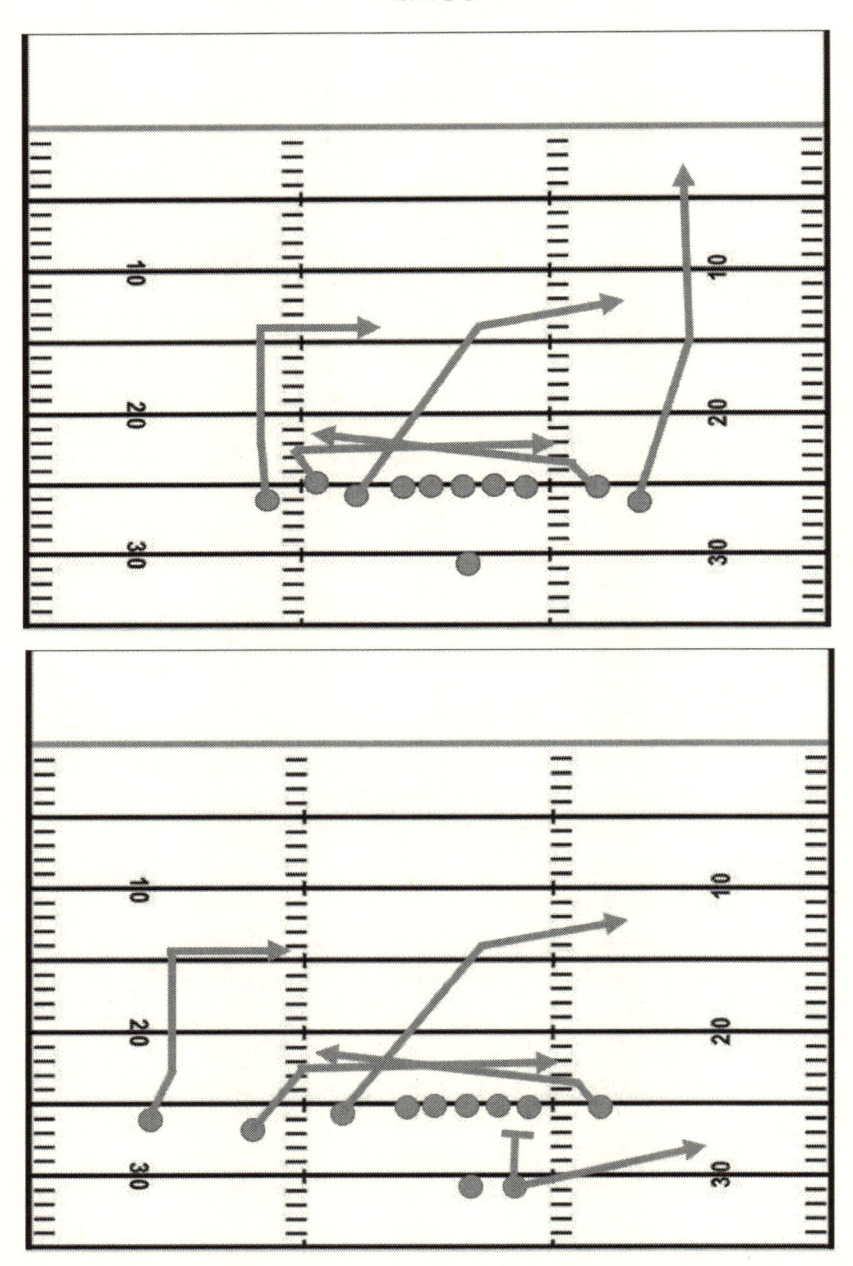

The 2018 Los Angeles Chargers Passing Index

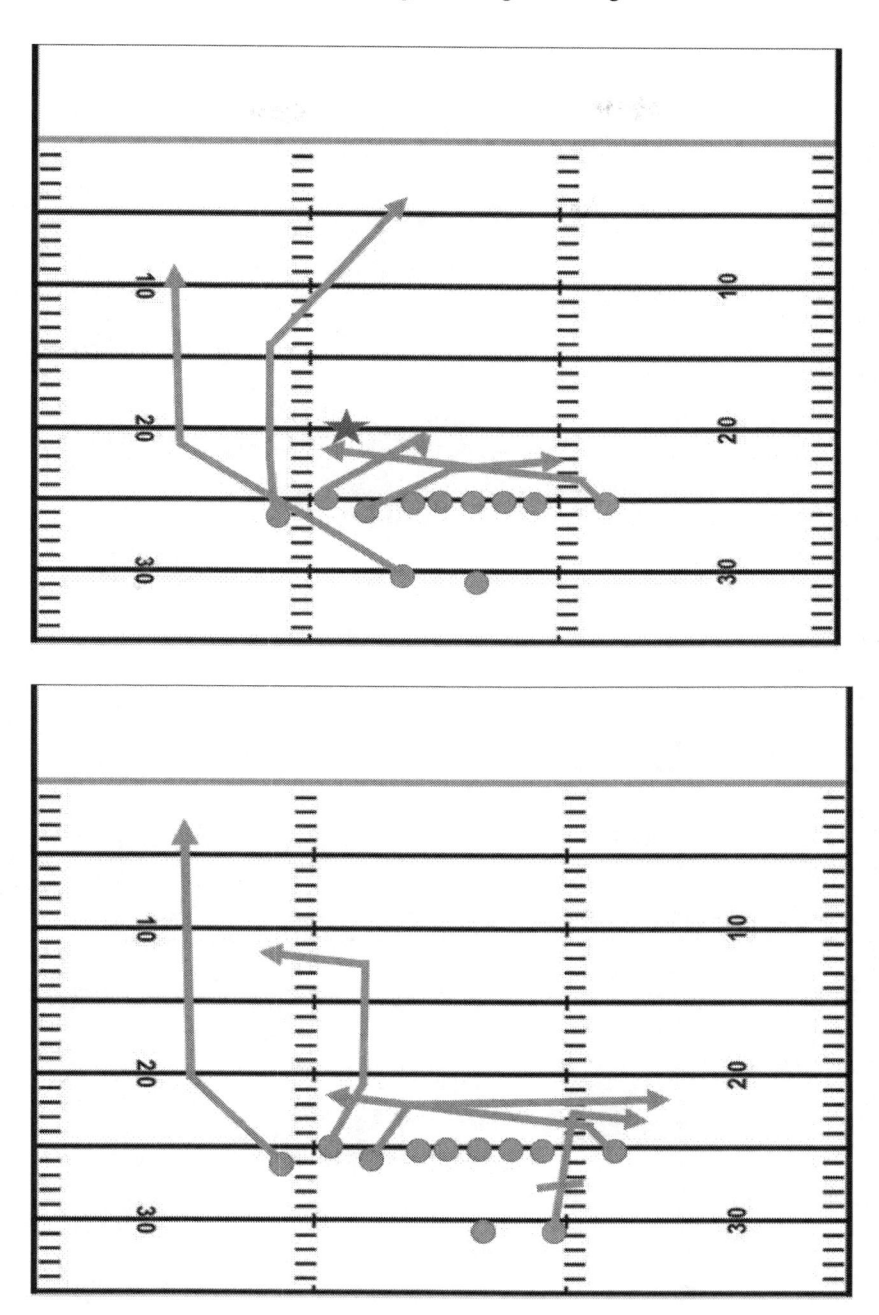

129

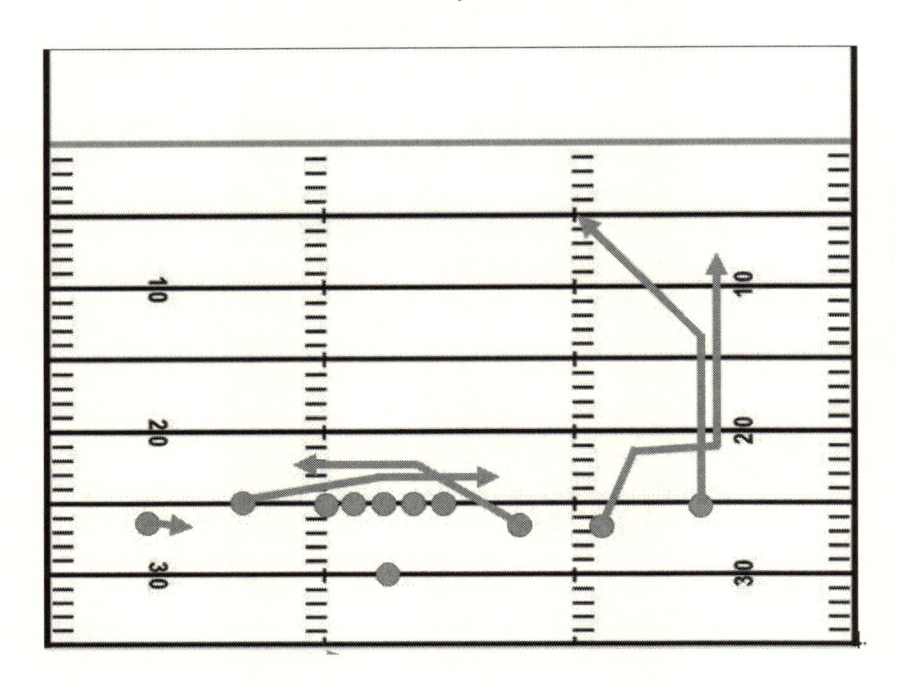

Average Yards per Play	6.4

1st Down		Third Down (includes RZ)	
Called	Average	Called	Success Rate
3	11.7	8	63%
2nd Down 6-1		2nd Down 7+	
Called	Average	Called	Average
1	0.0	3	0.0
Red Zone 10-0		Red Zone 10-20	
Called	Touchdown %	Called	Touchdown %
1	0%	1	0%

The 2018 Los Angeles Chargers Passing Index

Week	Quarter	Time	Down	ToGo	Location	Yards
Week 1 vs KC	4	15:00	2	5	LAC 34	0
Week 3 vs LAR	3	11:56	2	8	LAC 27	0
Week 3 vs LAR	4	14:17	3	4	RAM 29	5
Week 5 vs OAK	3	6:48	3	4	RAI 15	3
Week 6 vs CLE	1	6:23	3	6	LAC 8	0
Week 7 vs TEN	4	7:33	3	11	LAC 40	11
Week 9 vs SEA	2	2:05	1	10	LAC 35	12
Week 11 vs DEN	2	11:21	2	8	LAC 15	0
Week 11 vs DEN	2	3:25	3	4	DEN 33	29
Week 11 vs DEN	4	10:02	1	10	DEN 44	23
Week 13 vs PIT	4					2
Week 16 vs BAL	1	11:22	3	2	LAC 33	0
Week 16 vs BAL	3	0:22	3	4	LAC 18	5
Week 16 vs BAL	4	10:59	3	6	LAC 30	12
Week 17 vs DEN	1	14:14	1	10	DEN 43	0
DIV vs NE	2	9:31	2	10	LAC 49	0

RB & TE Slow Screens

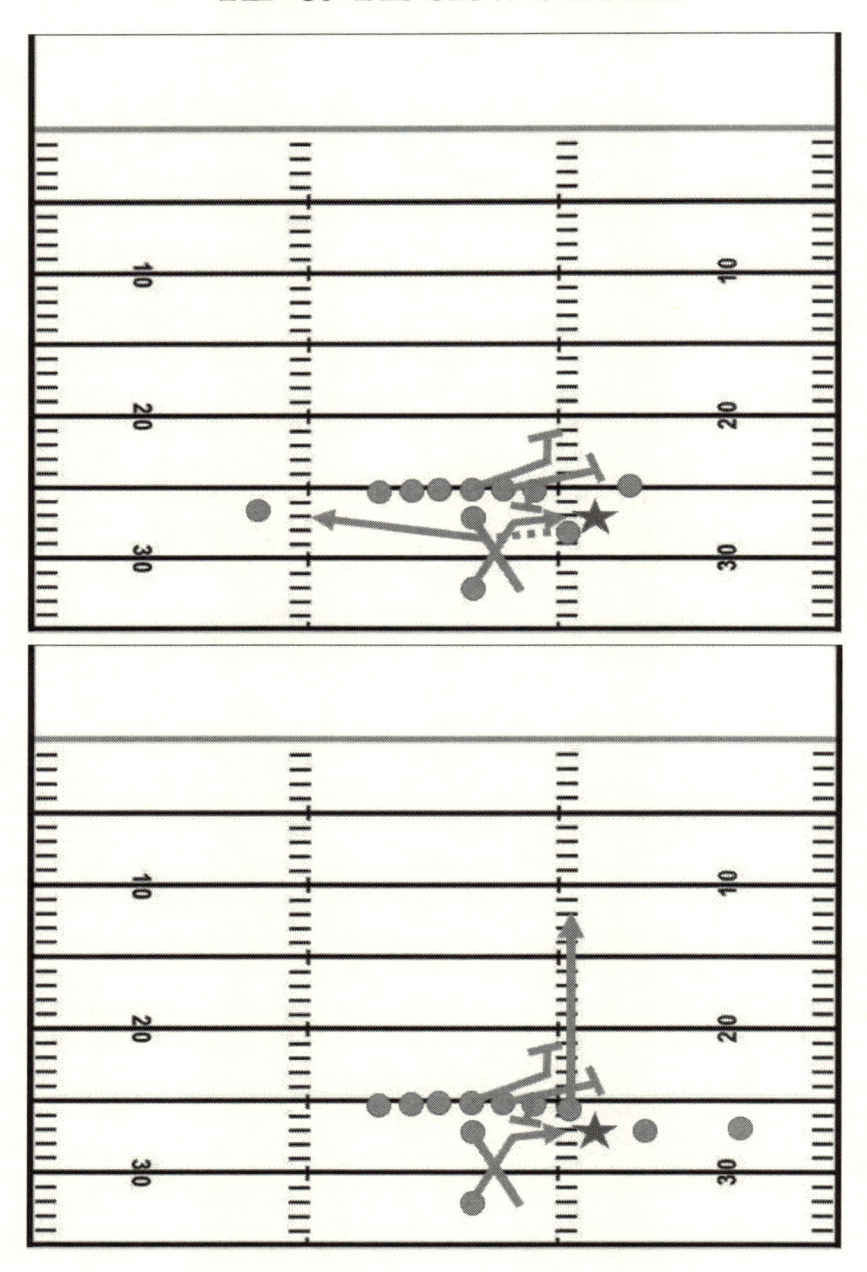

The 2018 Los Angeles Chargers Passing Index

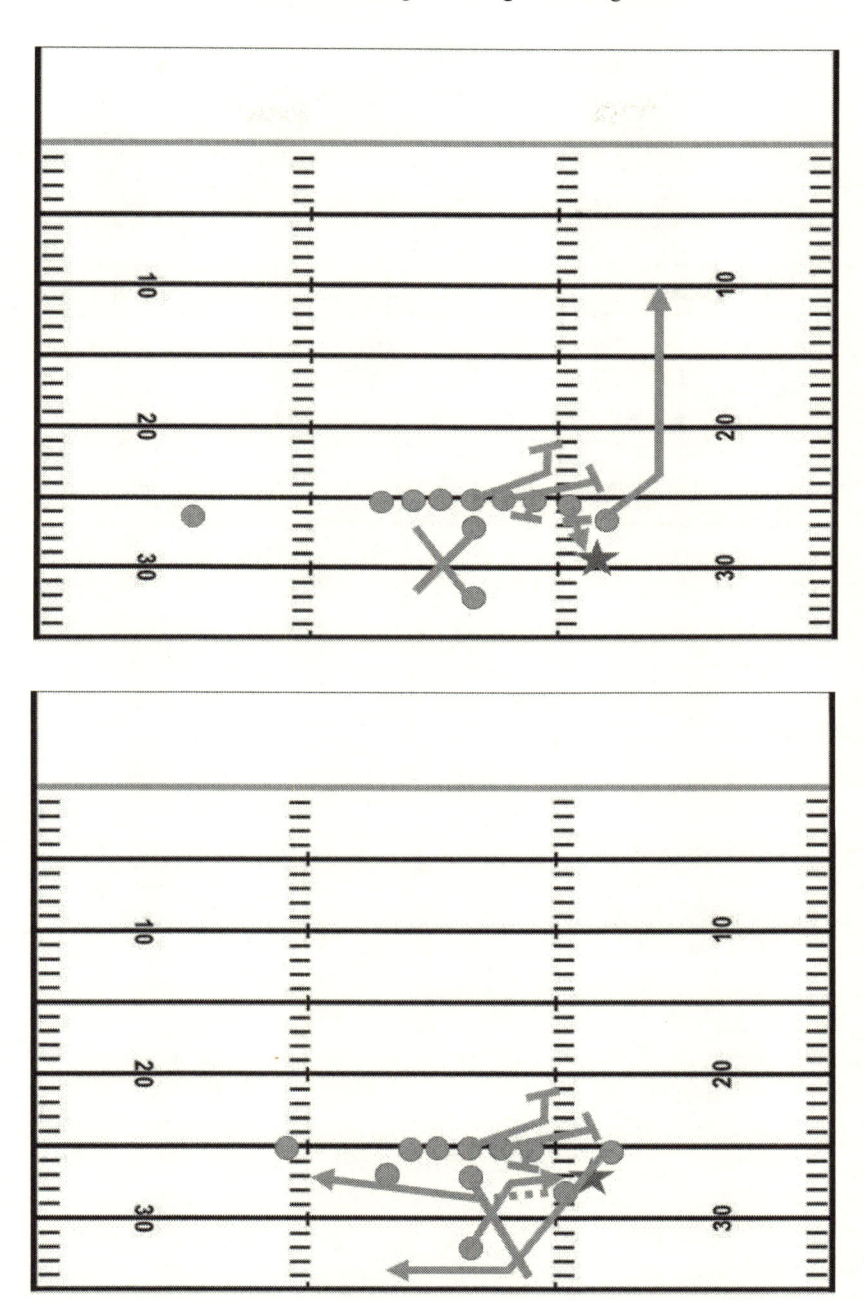

Average Yards per Play	6.6

1st Down		Third Down (includes RZ)	
Called	Average	Called	Success Rate
3	0.7	3	33%
2nd Down 6-1 |||| 2nd Down 7+	
Called	Average	Called	Average
3	11.3	8	7.6
Red Zone 10-0 |||| Red Zone 10-20	
Called	Touchdown %	Called	Touchdown %
0	0%	5	20%

Week	Quarter	Time	Down	ToGo	Location	Yards
Week 1 vs KC	1	2:00	2	9	KAN 28	-2
Week 1 vs KC	4	13:01	1	10	KAN 28	2
Week 1 vs KC	4	1:40	3	10	KAN 28	-2
Week 2 vs BUF	2	8:41	1	10	LAC 19	0
Week 2 vs BUF	4	6:22	2	9	BUF 15	5
Week 3 vs LAR	3	14:20	2	4	LAC 31	0
Week 5 vs OAK	2	2:48	2	6	RAI 44	34
Week 5 vs OAK	4	9:51	2	4	RAI 13	13
Week 6 vs CLE	1	6:26	2	6	LAC 8	0
Week 7 vs TEN	3	8:55	2	9	LAC 26	11
Week 9 vs SEA	2	5:08	2	8	LAC 43	0
Week 10 vs OAK	3	8:21	2	9	LAC 26	5
Week 10 vs OAK	4	8:38	2	6	RAI 17	-5
Week 11 vs DEN	2	5:31	3	7	LAC 29	32
Week 12 vs ARI	3	5:59	2	10	LAC 27	15
Week 13 vs PIT	4	12:00	1	10	LAC 21	0
Week 14 vs CIN	1	0:04	2	11	CIN 26	21
Week 15 vs KC	2	11:31	2	18	KAN 21	8
Week 16 vs BAL	1	6:20	2	7	LAC 46	3
Week 16 vs BAL	1	5:00	3	19	LAC 34	0
Week 16 vs BAL	2	0:55	2	10	RAV 20	0
Week 12 vs ARI	2	15:00	2	14	CRD 14	5

Tunnel Screens

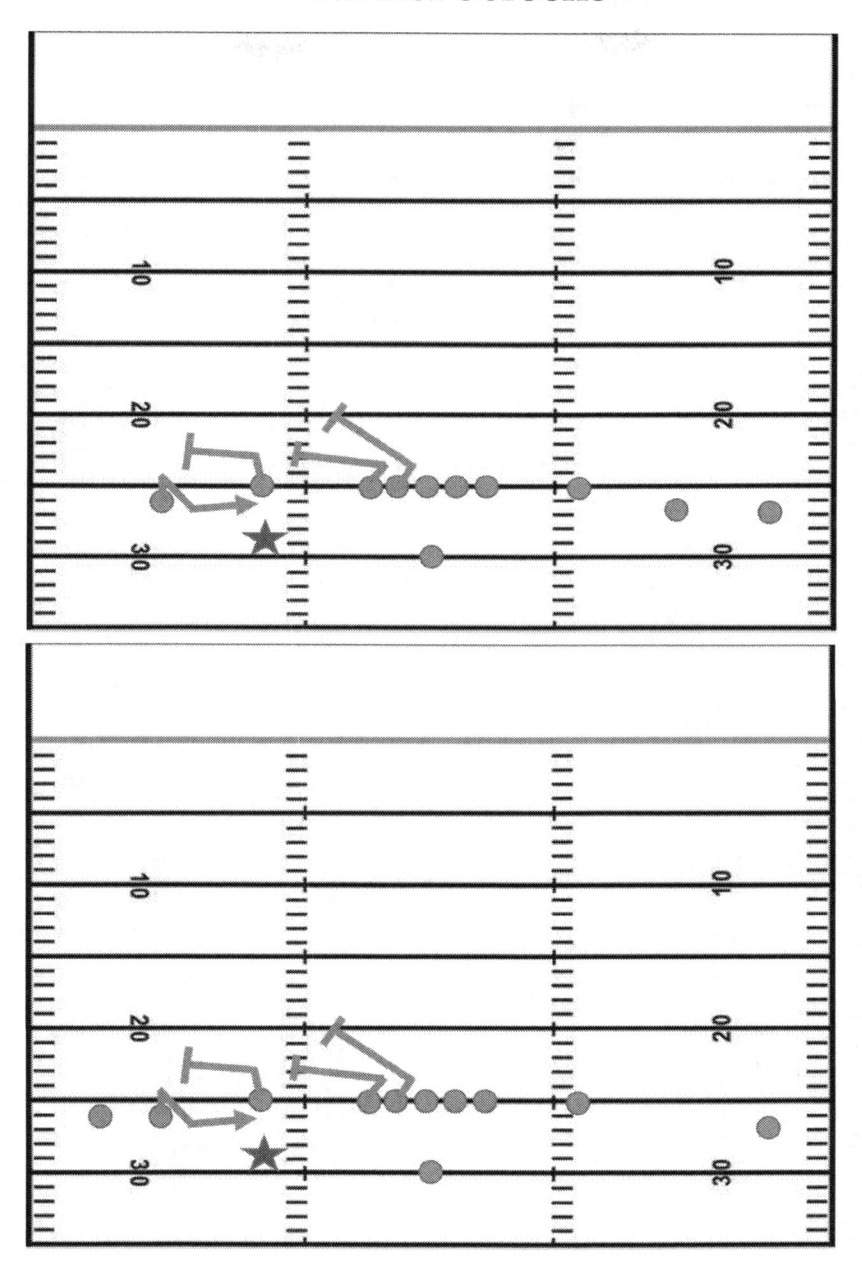

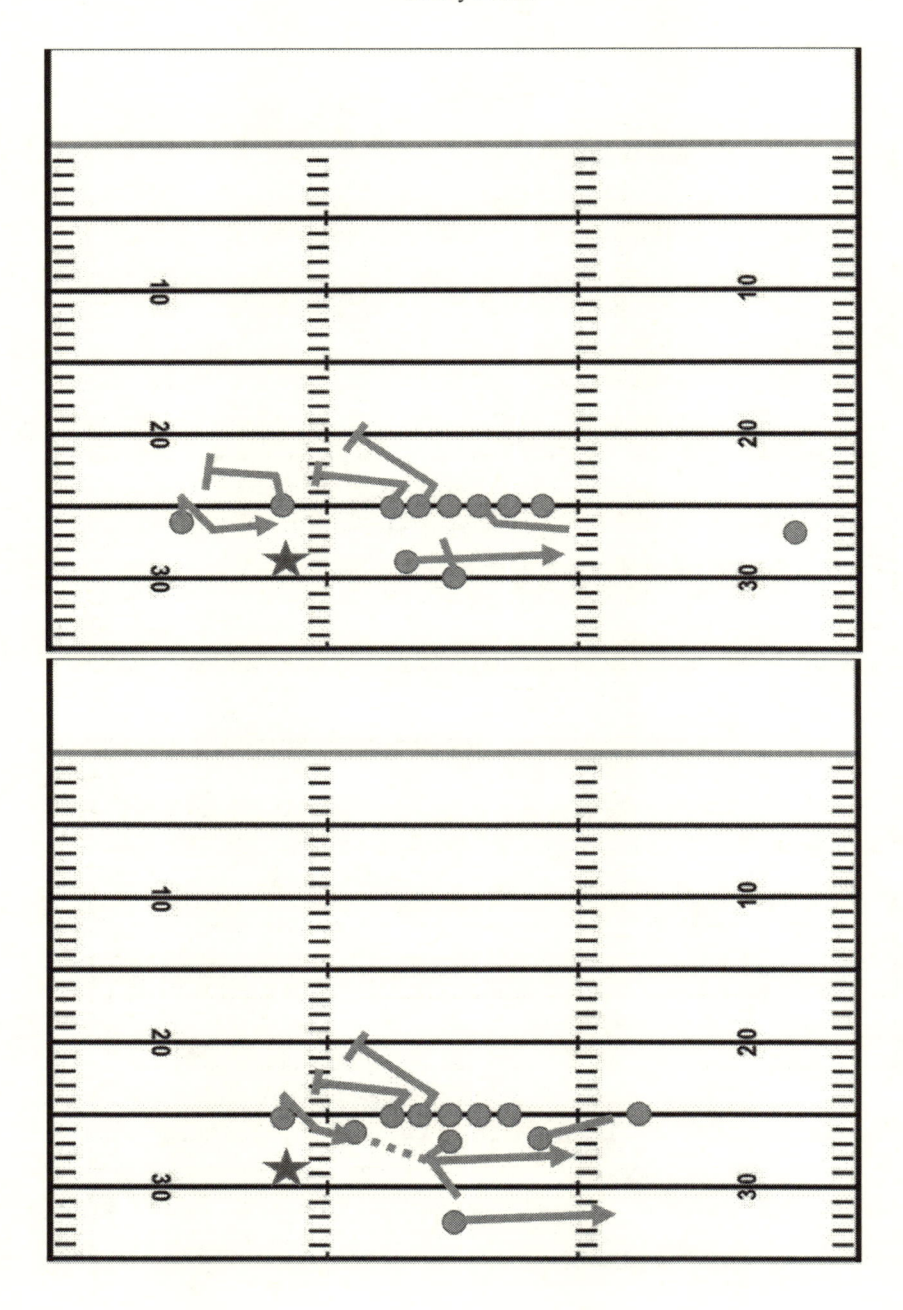

Bobby Peters

The 2018 Los Angeles Chargers Passing Index

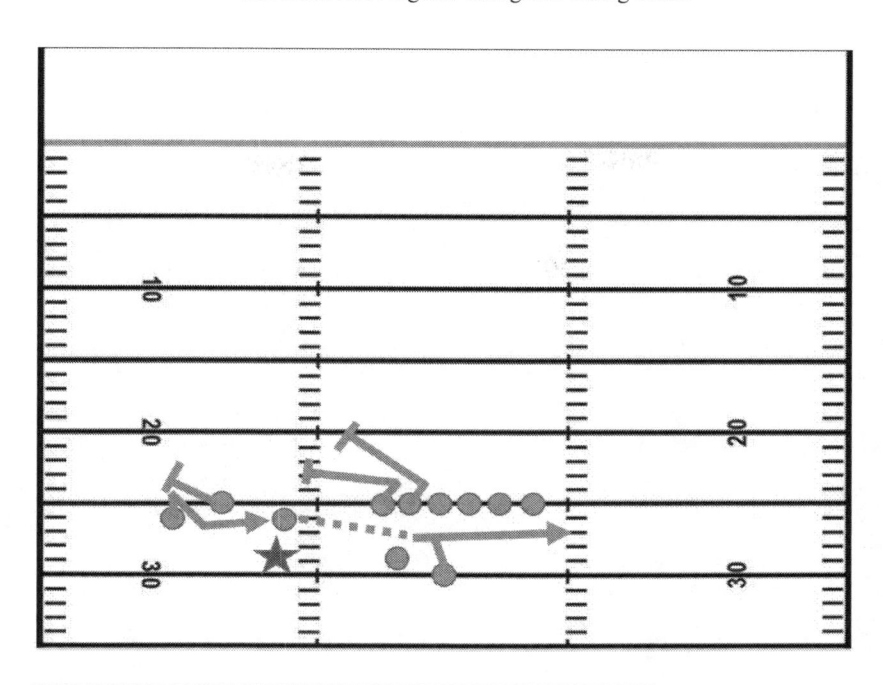

Average Yards per Play	4.9

1st Down	
Called	Average
4	9.8
2nd Down 6-1	
Called	Average
1	1.0
Red Zone 10-0	
Called	Touchdown %
1	0%

Third Down (includes RZ)	
Called	Success Rate
7	29%
2nd Down 7+	
Called	Average
3	2.3
Red Zone 10-20	
Called	Touchdown %
0	0%

Week	Quarter	Time	Down	ToGo	Location	Yards
Week 1 vs KC	2	1:27	2	5	LAC 30	1
Week 4 vs SF	4	7:47	3	3	SFO 3	0
Week 5 vs OAK	1	4:11	3	10	RAI 44	-1
Week 5 vs OAK	4	15:00	1	20	LAC 42	12
Week 6 vs CLE	2	10:05	3	22	LAC 31	0
Week 6 vs CLE	2	2:00	1	10	LAC 37	16
Week 6 vs CLE	3	5:30	1	10	CLE 44	0
Week 11 vs DEN	1	8:18	2	25	DEN 35	4
Week 11 vs DEN	3	3:55	3	9	DEN 35	TO
Week 11 vs DEN	4	7:27	3	15	DEN 26	14
Week 11 vs DEN	4	2:00	3	7	DEN 48	0
Week 12 vs ARI	2	8:30	1	10	CRD 38	11
Week 14 vs CIN	2	11:27	2	12	LAC 5	0
Week 15 vs KC	2	1:14	2	15	KAN 27	3
WC vs BAL	2	0:15	3	7	RAV 32	9

Red Zone Play Action Specials

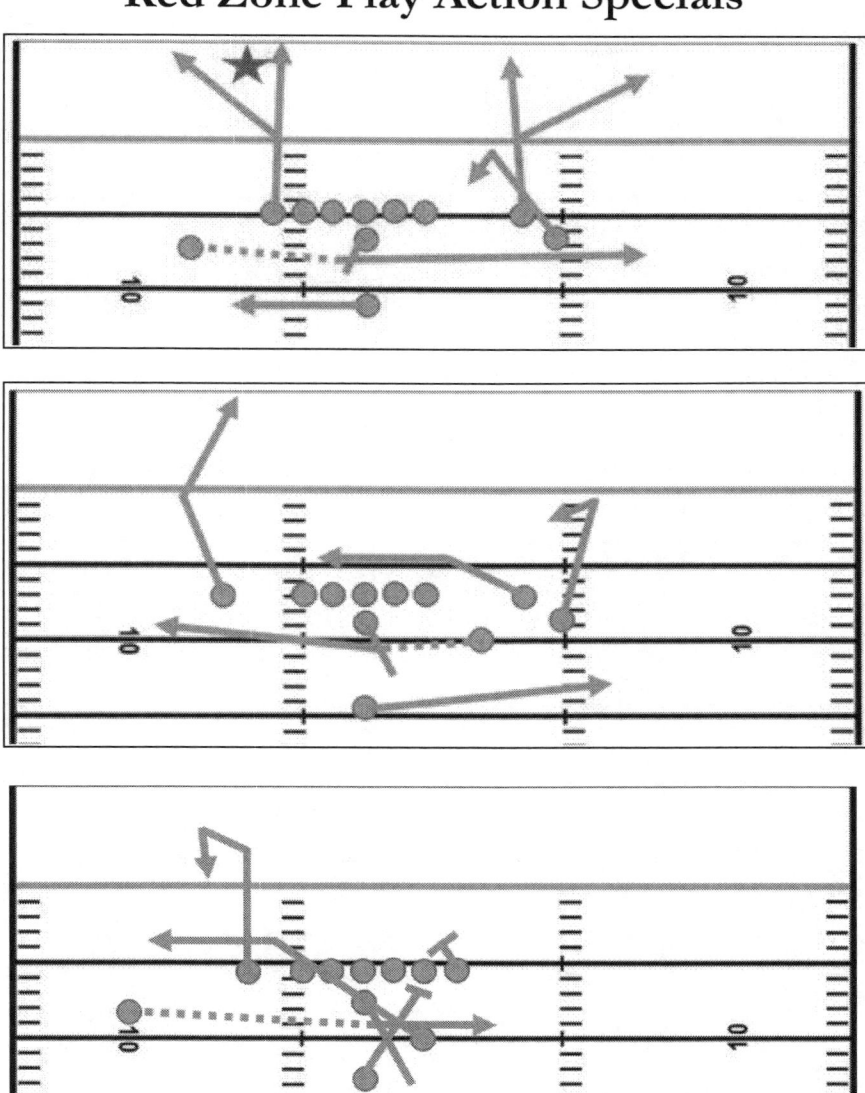

Bobby Peters

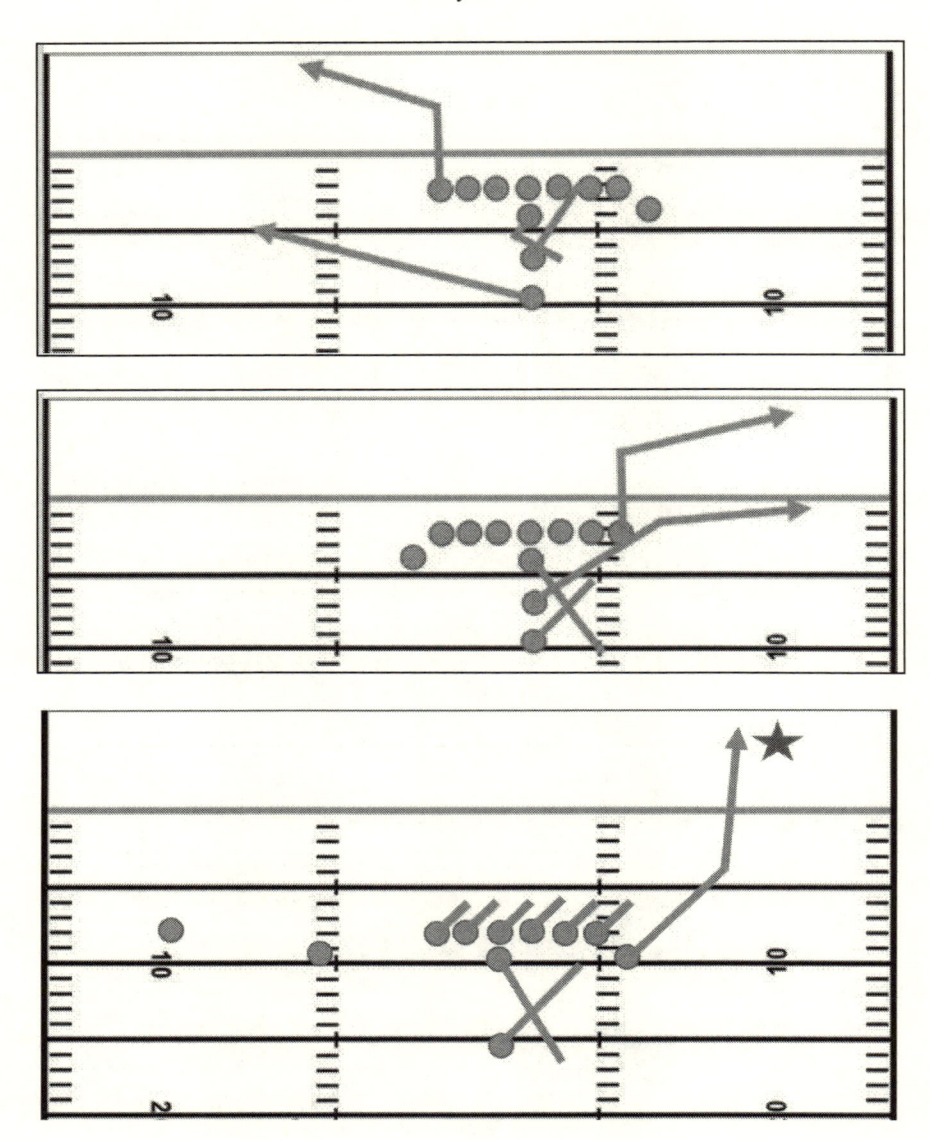

The 2018 Los Angeles Chargers Passing Index

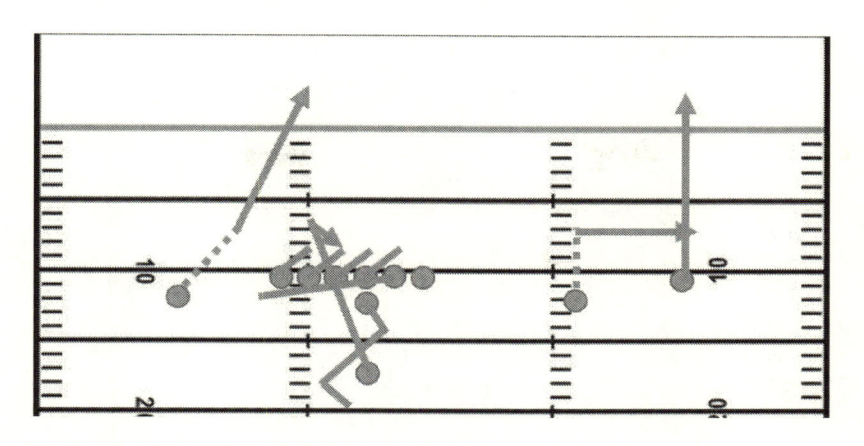

Average Yards per Play	3.2

1st Down		Third Down (includes RZ)	
Called	Average	Called	Success Rate
0	0.0	0	0%
2nd Down 6-1		2nd Down 7+	
Called	Average	Called	Average
0	0.0	0	0.0
Red Zone 10-0		Red Zone 10-20	
Called	Touchdown %	Called	Touchdown %
11	36%	1	0%

Week	Quarter	Time	Down	ToGo	Location	Yards
Week 2 vs BUF	2	10:49	2	5	BUF 9	9
Week 2 vs BUF	2	2:48	2	10	BUF 10	8
Week 4 vs SF	1	1:37	1	4	SFO 4	-1
Week 4 vs SF	4	8:31	2	8	SFO 8	5
Week 4 vs SF	4	2:25	2	5	SFO 14	10
Week 7 vs TEN	4	12:41	2	6	OTI 10	0
Week 9 vs SEA	2	11:36			SEA 2	0
Week 10 vs OAK	2	6:42	2	6	RAI 8	-1
Week 12 vs ARI	3	8:09	1	4	CRD 4	4
Week 13 vs PIT	3	1:43			PIT 2	2
WC vs BAL	3	0:11	2	2	RAV 2	1
DIV vs NE	4	7:42	1	1	NWE 1	1

Other Misc. Play Calls

Week	Play #	Play Call	Quarter	Time	Yards
Week 1 vs KC	41	2x2 Drive	4	5:56	0
Week 4 vs SF	19	2x2 Drive	2	3:54	16
Week 16 vs BAL	28	2x2 Drive	4	12:19	-2
Week 7 vs TEN	22	4 Man Scissors	4	13:22	4
Week 15 vs KC	39	Bison - Whip	4	1:18	0
Week 2 vs BUF	30	Bison Variation	4	5:44	9
Week 2 vs BUF	32	Bison Variation	4	3:57	0
Week 9 vs SEA	13	Dagger Corner	2	5:03	0
WC vs BAL	27	Dagger Corner	3	3:43	0
DIV vs NE	8	Dagger Corner	2	11:01	0
Week 6 vs CLE	18	Deep Over	3	8:06	20
Week 11 vs DEN	28	Double Cross	3	15:00	19
Week 3 vs LAR	19	Double Move	3	10:25	6
WC vs BAL	7	Double Move	2	12:40	17
Week 3 vs LAR	10	Double Post HB Burst	2	6:23	0
Week 16 vs BAL	7	F Cross	2	10:53	11
Week 12 vs ARI	23	Fade	2	0:13	2
Week 12 vs ARI	24	Fake Jet Dagger H Rail	3	14:08	16
Week 15 vs KC	15	Fake Jet Rollout	2	2:18	3
Week 7 vs TEN	19	Fake Jet Scissors	3	1:22	-1
Week 9 vs SEA	15	Fake Jet Scissors (creative)	2	2:00	0
Week 12 vs ARI	5	Fake Now Screen	1	1:58	4
WC vs BAL	14	H Post	2	3:35	0
Week 3 vs LAR	24	H Post	3	0:33	-4
Week 1 vs KC	33	H Post Double Move	4	12:09	20
Week 11 vs DEN	32	H Post Z COP	3	10:32	6
Week 7 vs TEN	17	Hitches	3	2:41	0
Week 16 vs BAL	23	Hitches	3	0:56	5
WC vs BAL	4	Hitches Spot	1	3:21	2
WC vs BAL	25	Hitches Spot	3	10:37	8
Week 14 vs CIN	28	Hitches X Go	3	1:16	0
Week 15 vs KC	22	Hitches Y Whip	3	8:47	4
Week 1 vs KC	21	Man Pick Play	3	9:18	11
Week 1 vs KC	25	Man Pick Play	3	0:42	20
Week 1 vs KC	40	Man Pick Play	4	6:32	8
Week 4 vs SF	23	Man Pick Play	2	0:47	2
Week 5 vs OAK	17	Man Pick Play	3	11:20	17
Week 13 vs PIT	16	Man Pick Play	2	3:56	0
WC vs BAL	32	Man Pick Play	4	14:44	2

The 2018 Los Angeles Chargers Passing Index

Week	Play #	Play Call	Quarter	Time	Yards
Week 1 vs KC	17	Max Fades	2	7:47	0
Week 3 vs LAR	22	Max Fades	3	1:11	0
Week 15 vs KC	35	Max Fades	4	4:03	0
Week 12 vs ARI	9	Mesh	2	11:17	-5
Week 6 vs CLE	1	PA Comeback	1	12:46	4
Week 15 vs KC	10	PA Curl Swirl	2	8:03	14
Week 2 vs BUF	13	PA Curl Wheel	2	6:27	7
Week 14 vs CIN	27	PA Curl Wheel	3	2:42	6
DIV vs NE	12	PA Double Cross	2	5:59	26
Week 9 vs SEA	2	PA F Cross	1	4:56	11
Week 7 vs TEN	9	PA Max Deep Hitches	3	15:00	13
Week 16 vs BAL	20	PA Max Double Move	3	5:36	1
Week 6 vs CLE	10	PA Max U Corner Z Post	2	6:43	45
Week 9 vs SEA	6	PA Max Verticals	2	12:40	0
Week 16 vs BAL	1	PA Max Verticals	1	14:55	TO
Week 6 vs CLE	9	PA Max X Corner Z Post	2	7:46	44
Week 1 vs KC	23	PA Quick Dig	3	7:13	16
Week 10 vs OAK	28	PA Rollout	4	4:10	4
Week 11 vs DEN	45	PA Rollout	4	3:38	1
WC vs BAL	1	PA Rollout	1	11:54	0
WC vs BAL	35	PA Rollout	4	5:01	-1
Week 15 vs KC	24	PA Throwback	3	2:53	11
Week 9 vs SEA	20	Pin - Drag	3	12:44	0
Week 4 vs SF	2	Pin - Whip	1	14:12	TO
Week 4 vs SF	8	QB Sneak	1	9:37	1
Week 2 vs BUF	20	Quads Hitch Spacing	3	9:12	0
Week 14 vs CIN	24	Quads Z Curl	3	7:51	0
Week 1 vs KC	22	RB Swing Screen (creative)	3	8:38	20
Week 1 vs KC	11	Scat Variation	2	11:57	0
Week 1 vs KC	15	Scissors	2	7:58	0
Week 17 vs DEN	10	Scissors	1	4:25	TO
Week 14 vs CIN	14	Scissors - Drag	2	4:50	0
Week 14 vs CIN	22	Scissors - Drag	3	9:18	7
Week 1 vs KC	48	Scissors COP	4	1:57	12
Week 1 vs KC	49	Scissors COP	4	1:51	0
Week 4 vs SF	1	Shallow	1	15:00	0
Week 13 vs PIT	12	Spot	2	9:09	14
Week 2 vs BUF	18	Spot - Slants	2	2:00	2
Week 1 vs KC	28	Spot - Verticals	4	14:57	25
WC vs BAL	20	Spot Slants	2	0:29	3
Week 4 vs SF	10	Spot Variation	1	7:11	0
Week 15 vs KC	43	Fades	4	0:08	1
Week 10 vs OAK	8	Stick Nod	2	5:55	0
Week 7 vs TEN	2	Stick Swirl	1	6:55	11

Bobby Peters

Week	Play #	Play Call	Quarter	Time	Yards
Week 12 vs ARI	25	Trick Play	3	12:12	-10
Week 17 vs DEN	23	Veritcals F Whip	4	12:35	0
Week 5 vs OAK	11	Verticals	2	7:58	0
Week 13 vs PIT	11	Verticals	2	9:57	0
Week 13 vs PIT	34	Verticals	4	10:26	19
Week 9 vs SEA	7	Verticals - Curl	2	12:32	0
Week 12 vs ARI	17	Verticals - Spot	2	1:00	11
Week 16 vs BAL	25	Verticals - Spot	4	15:00	0
Week 11 vs DEN	12	Verticals - Whip	1	1:27	0
Week 13 vs PIT	8	Verticals - Whip	1	3:14	9
Week 9 vs SEA	5	Verticals - Z Under	1	0:01	12
Week 9 vs SEA	28	Verticals X Double Move	4	8:05	0
Week 15 vs KC	30	Verticals Y Whip	4	7:03	14
Week 14 vs CIN	6	Z Curl	1	3:41	-7

ABOUT THE AUTHOR

Bobby currently coaches at York Community High School, in Elmhurst Illinois. You can find more of his work at:

www.theofficialpetersreport.blogspot.com

Email: bpeters1212@gmail.com

Other Books on Amazon

The 2018 Chicago Bears Complete Offensive Manual

The 2017 Los Angeles Rams Third Down Manual

The 2017 Philadelphia Eagles Third Down Manual

The Melting Pot: How to Acclimate Old NFL Concepts into Your High School or College Offense

Quarterback Development: How Four NFL Teams Coached Their Quarterback to Have A Successful 2016 Season

The Complete Third Down Manual: The 2016 New Orleans Saints

Made in the USA
San Bernardino, CA
11 May 2019